Accounting for Growth in Latin America and the Caribbean

Accounting for Growth in Latin America and the Caribbean

Improving Corporate Financial Reporting to Support Regional Economic Development

Henri Fortin
Ana Cristina Hirata Barros
Kit Cutler

THE WORLD BANK
Washington, D.C.

ISBN: 978-0-8213-8108-3
eISBN: 978-0-8213-8111-3
DOI: 10.1596/978-0-8213-8108-3

Library of Congress Cataloging-in-Publication Data

Accounting for growth in Latin America and the Caribbean : improving corporate financial reporting to support regional economic development / Henri Fortin, Ana Cristina Hirata Barros, Kit Cutler.
    p. cm. — (Directions in development)
  Includes bibliographical references and index.
  ISBN 978-0-8213-8108-3 — ISBN 978-0-8213-8111-3 (electronic)
  1. Accounting—Latin America. 2. Accounting—Caribbean Area. 3. Corporations—Latin America—Accounting. 4. Corporations—Caribbean Area—Accounting. 5. Economic development—Latin America. 6. Economic development—Caribbean Area. I. Fortin, Henri, 1964– II. Hirata Barros, Ana Cristina, 1973– III. Cutler, Kit, 1979–
  HF5616.L29A33 2009
  657.098—dc22

                                                    2009035880

Cover image by: Imagezoo/Images.com/Corbis.
Cover design: Naylor Design, Inc.

Contents

Boxes

Figures

Tables

Foreword

Countries in Latin America and the Caribbean (LAC) are better positioned than in the past to realize their development potential. Since 2000, most countries in the region have tamed inflation, brought their external debt under control, and instituted more flexible exchange rate regimes. Domestic savings have contributed to financing rising investment while productivity gains have been an engine of growth in competitive sectors. In the past, external shocks spread quickly through much of the region, causing rapid currency devaluation and rising inflation—and leaving the poor much worse off. But the region learned from past crises, and the most striking evidence of this newly gained resilience is LAC's relatively better performance during the current global financial crisis compared with Eastern Europe and East Asia.

With countries such as Brazil and Mexico emerging as global players, the region is becoming part of the solution to global challenges ranging from the financial crisis to global climate change. This typically middle-income region managed to lift 60 million people from poverty between 2002 and 2008, a trend that is now threatened by the effects of the global crisis.

There is no model, nor a blueprint, that can signal a development path for the whole region. Within a diverse region, each nation is trying to find its own way to economic and social well-being. What is clear is that Latin Americans want a future that offers opportunities for all citizens, not only for a few.

To make this dream a reality, the region must modernize its infrastructure, improve the quality of the education system, enhance the business climate, and make the state work for the people by providing basic services to all citizens.

This book focuses on the role of strong and transparent accounting and auditing systems in supporting these objectives. They represent an essential building block for any strategy directed toward achieving shared growth. Financial institutions, investors, corporate managers, regulatory authorities, and policy makers rely on sound financial information to make informed decisions. Moreover, as the financial crisis has demonstrated, financial stability is crucial in maintaining confidence in the economic system and providing the right signals for a quick recovery. Financial transparency is critical for market discipline to work and regulatory oversight to be effective as well as to facilitate the region's reemergence as an attractive destination for investors, particularly in the aftermath of the current crisis.

The World Bank works with countries in the region to advance their own reform processes to design and align their local accounting and auditing processes with international codes and standards of good practice. After eight years of studying the current state of accounting and auditing in individual countries and providing technical assistance at the national level, we felt it was useful to take a step back and see what could be learned from a broader, regional analysis. This book started from that premise, and the approach has borne fruit. This publication not only provides regional policy makers the opportunity to see where their country leads and where it lags, but it also helps to prioritize the challenges ahead and to shape the corporate financial reporting policy agenda of the future.

Pamela Cox
Vice President
Latin America and Caribbean Region
World Bank

Preface

Professional accountants play a key role in today's world. Accounting expertise is critical to enable businesses, large or small, to manage their operations effectively, access finance, and make properly informed decisions on a broad range of activities (investing, launching new products, recruiting, mitigating operational risks, and so on).

Accountants working in the public sector help ensure that the people's money is managed and spent efficiently, effectively, and transparently through strong country systems of public financial management. Accountants in state-owned enterprises help ensure that the company's "owners"—that is, citizens—get the best value from the enterprise. When acting as independent auditors, accountants uphold the public interest, and their work helps protect investors and other stakeholders.

Today, as global markets intertwine and financial innovations flourish, accounting and auditing have become ever more sophisticated. What was once largely a transaction-processing function, heavy on bookkeeping, is now a more analytic one. With the emergence of new, complex, and risky transactions, especially financial derivatives, new skills (such as risk-management consulting) have become necessary.

As countries in Latin America and the Caribbean (LAC) work to build a business climate that is conducive to private sector development and economic growth, they need to foster the development of the accounting and auditing profession as part of that effort. International standards must be promulgated and enforced by effective regulators; accountants' new and expanded role requires higher standards of education and training; the profession must hold its members to demanding standards of quality and ethics; the LAC region's stakeholders must be brought into the international standard-setting dialogue. As this book details, there have already been success stories from all around the region in this realm.

This book is an effort to identify and promote these successes in the practice of reliable accounting and auditing, as well as to point out some missteps, so that the countries of the LAC region can collectively gain from their common experience. The lessons learned from this experience will surely be useful to partner countries in other regions, which may be at different points along the same path.

The World Bank will continue to be a steadfast partner for any policy maker who wishes to work toward reform in line with international good practices. This book is a small part of that partnership—an effort to show what we have learned in this area alongside our clients and in active consultation with the broader global community.

Stefan G. Koeberle
Director, Strategy and Operations
Latin America and Caribbean Region
World Bank

Elizabeth O. Adu
Director, Operational Services
Latin America and Caribbean Region
World Bank

Anthony Hegarty
Chief Financial Management Officer and
Head, Financial Management Sector Board
World Bank

Acknowledgments

The authors would like to offer special recognition and thanks to Jamil Sopher for his guidance at every step along the way from idea to finished book, his tough but insightful comments on innumerable drafts, and his accumulated wisdom from previous authorship and decades at the Bank. This book would not be what it is without his collaboration.

The authors are grateful to Roberto Tarallo for his leadership and overall guidance throughout the preparation of this book. For research assistance and contributions to various parts of the book, the authors would like to thank Alfred Borgonovo, Taiki Hirashima, David Martínez, David Nagy, Alfredo Rodríguez Neira, and Carlos Vicente.

An outstanding group of peer reviewers provided invaluable guidance and feedback that markedly improved the book: Héctor Alfonso, Aquiles Almansi, Sylvia Barrett, Eva Gutierrez, John Hegarty, Mimi Ladipo, Jennifer Thomson, and Erik van der Plaats. Michael Crawford, William Experton, and Cynthia Hobbs provided their expert insights on the accounting education chapter and accompanying recommendations. Patricia Rogers's editorial review greatly improved the book's readability.

The authors are grateful to all those who contributed—whether as team member, peer reviewer, or member of a country management unit—to the preparation of the 17 ROSC A&A reports in LAC, which served as the basis for the book's analysis. In particular, the authors would like to express their sincere gratitude for the logistical support provided by Gilma Unda, Marianella Rivadeneira, Edgar Molina, and our colleagues in country offices. Thank you for many jobs well done.

Finally, thank you to all those individuals whom we have not mentioned, but whose help we have enjoyed over the years. Although we have benefited from assistance from many corners, we take sole responsibility for this work and for any errors it may contain.

About the Authors

Henri Fortin is a senior financial management specialist in the Latin America and Caribbean Region at the World Bank. He leads the Reports on the Observance of Standards and Codes (ROSC) Accounting & Auditing (A&A) program in that region and has been the lead author for 20 country reports since 2003. He advises partner countries on implementing reforms and capacity development programs to bring their corporate financial reporting to par with international standards. He is also the World Bank's project manager for several related knowledge activities including the CReCER annual conferences on Accounting and Accountability for Regional Economic Growth in Latin America and the Caribbean. Mr. Fortin holds a master's degree in management from Ecole des Hautes Etudes Commerciales in Paris, France.

Ana Cristina Hirata Barros is a consultant in the Financial Management Unit of the Latin America and Caribbean Region at the World Bank. She has worked on a number of corporate sector accounting and auditing issues since 2004, particularly the ROSC program, as well as ROSC follow-up projects and activities in the Latin America and Caribbean and in the Europe and Central Asia Regions. Currently, her work focuses mainly on issues pertaining to state-owned enterprises, small and medium enterprises, and accounting education. Ms. Hirata Barros holds a master's degree in public policy, with a focus in international development policy, from Georgetown University, and a bachelor's degree in international relations from the University of Brasília, Brazil. Prior to joining the World Bank, she worked in Brazil and the United States in government relations consulting and export promotion.

Kit Cutler is a junior professional associate in the Financial Management Unit of the Latin America and Caribbean Region at the World Bank. He is responsible for research, writing, and translation for the unit's corporate financial reporting work program. He has co-authored ROSC A&A reports on Panama, Nicaragua, and the Eastern Caribbean States, and prepared post-ROSC technical assistance projects for El Salvador and Honduras. He also assisted with the Spanish-language translation of the *International Education Standards for Professional Accountants*. Previously, Mr. Cutler worked in Pakistan and the United States for the Urban Institute, in Paraguay with the U.S. Peace Corps, and in Washington, DC, for the National Council for International Visitors. He holds a bachelor's degree in history, with a certificate in Latin American Studies, from Princeton University.

Abbreviations

A&A	Accounting and auditing
ACCA	Association of Chartered Certified Accountants
AIC	Asociación Interamericana de Contabilidad (Inter-American Accounting Association)
AICPA	American Institute of Certified Public Accountants
BM&F BOVESPA	Bolsa de Valores, Mercadorias & Futuros de São Paulo (Brazil's Securities, Commodities, and Futures Exchange)
CAP	Country Action Plan
CFC	Conselho Federal de Contabilidade (Brazil's Federal Accounting Council)
CGA	Certified General Accountants Association of Canada
CPC	Contador Público Certificado
CPD	Continuing professional development
CReCER	Contabilidad y Responsabilidad para el Crecimiento Económico Regional (Accounting and Accountability for Regional Economic Growth)
CVPCPA	Consejo de Vigilancia de la Profesión de Contaduría Pública y de Auditoría (El Salvador's Accounting and Auditing Professional Oversight Board)

EU	European Union
FASB	Financial Accounting Standards Board (U.S.)
FIRST	Financial Sector Reform and Strengthening Initiative
GAAP	Generally Accepted Accounting Principles
GAAS	Generally Accepted Auditing Standards
GDP	Gross domestic product
G-20	Group of Twenty Finance Ministers and Central Bank Governors
IASB	International Accounting Standards Board
IBRACON	Instituto dos Auditores Independentes do Brasil (Brazil's Institute of Independent Auditors)
IDB	Inter-American Development Bank
IES	International Education Standards
IFAC	International Federation of Accountants
IFIAR	International Forum of Independent Audit Regulators
IFRS	International Financial Reporting Standards
IMCP	Instituto Mexicano de Contadores Públicos (Mexico's Institute of Public Accountants)
IMF	International Monetary Fund
ISA	International Standards on Auditing
LAC	Latin America and the Caribbean Region
MD&A	Management Discussion and Analysis
MIF	Multilateral Investment Fund
NSC	National Steering Committee
OECD	Organisation for Economic Co-operation and Development
OECS	Organisation of Eastern Caribbean States
PCAOB	Public Company Accounting Oversight Board (U.S.)
PIE	Public interest entity
PIOB	Public Interest Oversight Board
ROSC	Report on the Observance of Standards and Codes
SAI	Supreme audit institution
SEC	Securities and Exchange Commission (U.S.)
SME	Small and medium enterprise
SMO	Statement of Membership Obligations
SOE	State-owned enterprise
SVS	Superintendencia de Valores y Seguros (Chile's Securities and Insurance Commission)
UNCTAD	United Nations Conference on Trade and Development

UNCTAD–   Intergovernmental Working Group of Experts on
 ISAR   International Standards of Accounting and Reporting
UNESCPA Universidad Especializada del Contador Público Autorizado
            (Panama's Authorized Public Accountant Specialized
            University)

Overview

The Latin America and Caribbean (LAC) region comprises a diverse set of countries that nonetheless face common challenges—especially high inequality and volatile growth—that have historically contributed to high levels of poverty. In recent years, the LAC region has achieved significant progress on both of these challenges. As a result, between 2002 and 2008, almost 60 million people in the region were lifted out of poverty (measured at US$4 a day, adjusted for purchasing power parity), and 41 million left the ranks of extreme poverty (measured at US$2 a day). This progress is now threatened by a global economic and financial crisis that has spread to the region from the United States and Europe, bringing declining external demand, weakening commodity prices, financial contagion, and falling remittances. Although growth forecasts vary widely, and the effect of the crisis on the region's economies is not uniform, the World Bank has projected that the LAC region's economy will contract by 2.2 percent in 2009 (World Bank 2009a).

Financial Reporting at the Core of LAC's Development Agenda

Sound accounting, auditing, and reporting practices are essential for promoting sustainable and equitable private sector–led growth and strengthening governance and accountability. They promote the development of capital markets, facilitate access to finance for local enterprises (particularly small and medium enterprises, or SMEs), promote an improved business climate, further the integration of local companies in the world economy, reduce the risk of crises in the financial sector, and enable the efficient operation or privatization of state-owned enterprises (SOEs).

This book seeks to identify the broad trends and drivers for reform in the LAC region's corporate financial reporting practices, drawing on the Bank's experience from 17 Reports on the Observance of Standards and Codes (ROSC) on Accounting and Auditing (A&A). It showcases country success stories and distills lessons learned in priority areas for reform, with a view to maximizing the chances of success for a corporate financial reporting reform agenda.

The region's recent focus on strengthening its corporate financial reporting framework has already begun to yield significant results. For example, in Brazil, rules that promote stronger A&A among listed companies have contributed to the deepening of the capital markets. In Mexico, higher licensing standards have led to more confidence in the financial statements that accountants prepare or audit, as well as to greater regional integration within North America. In Chile, a well-planned conversion to International Financial Reporting Standards (IFRS), now under way, paves the way for an orderly adoption of the standards and the accompanying benefits of international integration, lower costs of capital, and a better business climate. Other countries, too, have embarked on significant reforms of their A&A regime and are realizing important benefits.

A Conceptual Framework

Strong corporate financial reporting systems are built on three pillars (figure 1):

- Setting adequate requirements
- Developing capacity to implement applicable rules
- Enforcing applicable standards effectively.

Adequate requirements are clear, comprehensive, consistent, fair, and up-to-date laws and regulations, as well as rigorous standards for A&A. Capacity to apply appropriate standards requires skilled accountants,

Figure 1 Three Pillars of Financial Reporting Systems

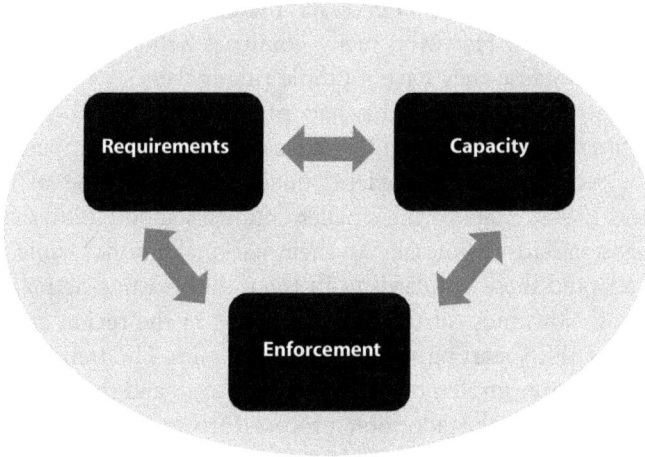

Source: Authors.

robust accounting education, and a system to maintain and upgrade skills on a continuing basis. A rigorous enforcement regime ensures compliance with the standards. These three pillars reinforce each other: setting requirements at the appropriate level makes enforcement easier and avoids unnecessarily stretching companies' capacity to comply. Indeed, adequate capacity of company accountants and auditors to follow rules and standards is a condition of compliance. Finally, imposing rules and standards without the corresponding enforcement actions ensures that the rules remain merely virtual.

Key Conclusions

This study finds that, while LAC countries have made significant progress in some areas, they could improve their corporate financial reporting systems with actions related to all three pillars.

Setting Adequate Rules:
A Robust Basis for Building Strong Frameworks
Over the last decades, LAC countries have built statutory frameworks for corporate financial reporting that are fairly complete; this is the area

where policy makers' attention has been most focused. Most countries have the legal flexibility to adapt their standards, even though the legislative and regulatory processes often do not match the speed of innovations in the private sector. However, many countries suffer from regulatory fragmentation because they have multiple rule makers.

Most countries in the region have adopted IFRS for listed companies, and Brazil has also adopted them for banks and insurance companies. The much-discussed "adopt versus adapt" dilemma is beginning to resolve itself. In the 1990s, many of the smaller countries adopted international accounting standards wholesale as their national norms, while larger countries adapted these standards to fit them into existing national rules and practices. Now, most of the large countries in the region are taking steps to adopt IFRS, starting with listed companies. The transition from adoption to effective implementation will take time, and the global financial crisis may delay the adoption process further in some countries. Nonetheless, it seems highly unlikely that LAC will change course; the momentum for adopting IFRS is a positive development for the region.

Two challenges that LAC policy makers face in setting adequate accounting and auditing requirements are SMEs and SOEs. LAC's SMEs are often subject to unduly stringent rules, which either increase the cost of doing business or foster a culture of noncompliance and informality. SMEs need a simplified accounting and financial reporting framework, with requirements commensurate with their size, the types of transactions they conduct, and their limited range of stakeholders. SOEs, for their part, pose inherently difficult and complex challenges, and LAC's policy makers often grapple with SOE reform. Good international practice and experience call for large SOEs to observe the same standards relating to accounting, auditing, reporting, and governance as listed companies: for example, applying IFRS, having annual independent audits, and making their financial statements public. Most LAC SOEs have yet to fulfill such requirements. (Figure 2 illustrates the concept of differentiated requirements.)

Developing Capacity to Apply the Rules: A Shared Role for Educators and Professional Bodies

Traditionally, universities have played a leading role in A&A education in LAC, and they will continue to do so. Most countries rely on a university degree as the primary if not the only condition to award the professional license of public accountant or statutory auditor. However, the various accounting curricula in LAC are of uneven quality and often outdated.

Figure 2 Setting Adequate Corporate Financial Reporting Requirements

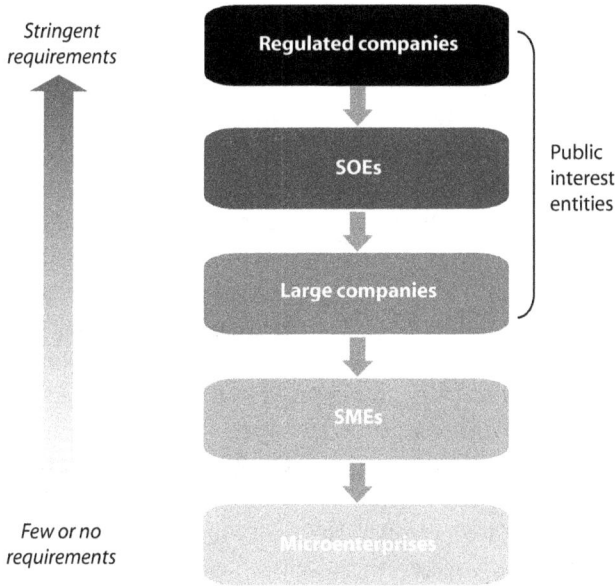

Source: Authors.

They do not reflect important issues that are considered essential to modern corporate financial reporting. Accounting professors in the region, for a variety of reasons, have difficulty keeping up to date with developments in the field, especially given the pace of change. Strengthening education and training will help sustain the momentum toward adopting IFRS and International Standards on Auditing (ISA).

The adoption of international standards has prompted universities and the profession to offer seminars, workshops, and other training courses on IFRS and ISA. An increasing number of professional accounting associations require their members to pursue continuing professional development (CPD), and more have voluntary requirements. These are important first steps.

Accounting professional bodies in the region play a leading role in working toward a stronger accounting profession that adheres to high standards of quality and ethics. Stronger organizations are more likely to have introduced CPD requirements and to have set a higher bar for becoming and remaining a qualified accountant. However, most professional bodies suffer from low revenues and high fixed costs. They also fear that imposing difficult standards will lead to member attrition and thus a less viable organization. These associations have tended to lag behind international good practice with respect to their rules on entry requirements, quality assurance, ethics, and so on.

This book suggests a demand-driven approach to building capacity within the profession in LAC, focusing on professional certification and accompanying measures to improve accounting education at the university level. A certification system culminating in a professional examination is one way to ensure that new entrants into the profession have a minimum level of qualification. The creation of robust certification requirements can also bring other indirect benefits, including increased demand for high-quality accounting education at the university level, heightened prestige of the accounting profession, and enhanced oversight of supervised entities. Creating such a system will require time and the mobilization of the accounting and auditing profession (for example, to administer the certification examination). In parallel, universities should seize the opportunity to revamp their accounting curricula to meet the requirements of professional certification.

Ensuring Compliance with the Rules

Compliance with financial reporting requirements remains a difficult area for all countries in LAC. Outside of the stock market, there are few incentives—and several disincentives—for companies to follow A&A rules. For example, many businesses perceive transparent reporting as a potential threat to their competitiveness. Many companies have traditionally been closely held within families and are not accustomed to disclosing financial information. Moreover, many business leaders are reluctant to comply with IFRS because they feel that the administrative burden of complying outweighs the benefits for their companies.

Financial sector regulatory agencies in LAC countries have improved their overall supervisory framework during the last decade in response to the lessons from a series of bank crises across the region. Banking supervisors, regulators of nonbank financial institutions, securities market regulators, and other regulatory agencies have generally adequate statutory enforcement powers, but they frequently lack the expertise to conduct effective enforcement of corporate financial reporting requirements.

On the auditing side, after a wave of corporate failures and scandals, a new model—the independent audit oversight body—has emerged at the international level to address the concern of "Who will guard the guardians?" These bodies, whose responsibilities range from registration of auditors to independent review of their work, have replaced self-regulation arrangements and are required in many countries, including the United States, European Union member states, and Japan (figure 3 illustrates such a model). LAC countries have generally not followed this trend, but the region is gradually moving in that direction. For example, Argentina, Brazil, the Dominican Republic, and El Salvador have put into place elements of an independent audit oversight system to replace or supplement the traditional professional self-regulation arrangements that have proved to be unsatisfactory on their own.

Establishing an effective independent audit oversight system requires addressing several challenges: funding, the role of the profession, and the scope and coverage of the system. Given the public interest in sound corporate financial reporting, governments have a vested interest in ensuring that auditors effectively discharge their functions in accordance with applicable professional and ethical standards. For the foreseeable future,

Figure 3 Enforcement Regimes: Varying Degrees of Public Accountability

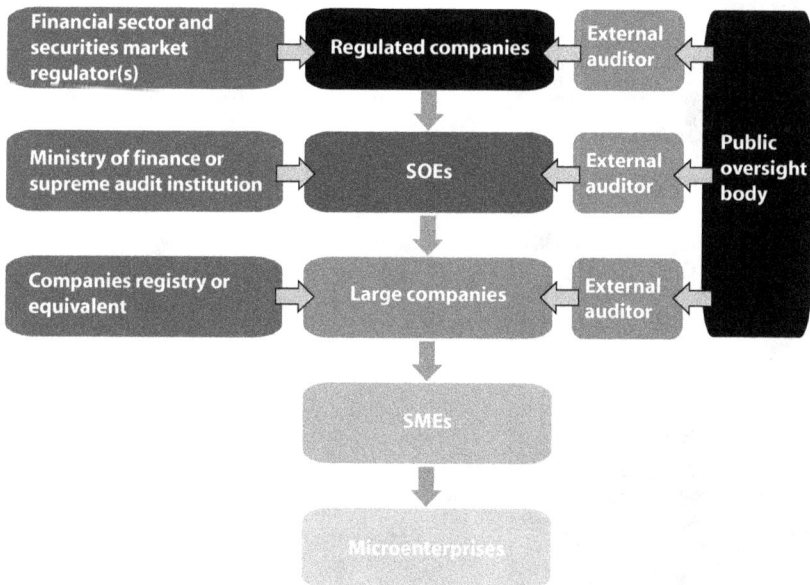

Source: Authors.

establishing independent audit oversight systems in LAC will likely require financial support from the national government's budget, as is the case in Japan and many European Union member states. There is a wide variation in approaches to developing a working model, and LAC will probably need to develop its own innovative solutions.

Looking Forward: A Roadmap for High-Quality Financial Reporting in LAC

To help countries identify the most urgent areas of reform, this book highlights four priority reforms within the three pillars of a strong corporate financial reporting framework (figure 4). None of the priority reforms is easy, but the authors consider that these are the reforms toward which policy makers should direct their energies to achieve the greatest impact with their limited resources.

Figure 4 Four Priority Reforms for Strong Corporate Financial Reporting Frameworks

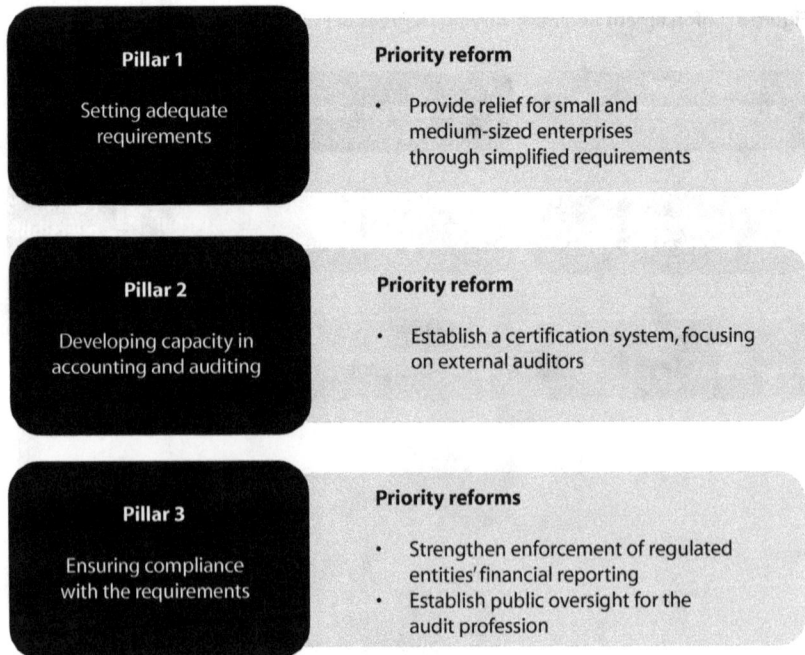

Pillar 1 Setting adequate requirements	Priority reform • Provide relief for small and medium-sized enterprises through simplified requirements
Pillar 2 Developing capacity in accounting and auditing	Priority reform • Establish a certification system, focusing on external auditors
Pillar 3 Ensuring compliance with the requirements	Priority reforms • Strengthen enforcement of regulated entities' financial reporting • Establish public oversight for the audit profession

Source: Authors.

The World Bank and other members of the donor community have a direct stake in corporate sector A&A reforms, which affect countries' development agendas. Several development agencies have already been providing technical assistance and capacity building through both lending and nonlending activities. The ROSC A&A reports—on which much of this book is based—are an important tool for assessing the region's progress in promoting common implementation of international standards. To implement the ROSC reports' policy recommendations, since 2005, the multidonor Financial Sector Reform and Strengthening (FIRST) Initiative has funded the preparation of country action plans in Chile, El Salvador, Honduras, and Peru to enhance those countries' financial reporting frameworks. The World Bank has also used information and communications technology to promote dialogue and the sharing of knowledge. Since 2006, it has used the Global Development Learning Network to organize a series of videoconference-based seminars in which leading specialists from around the world discuss specific A&A issues with participants from several LAC countries.

Finally, the financial crisis will likely result in renewed efforts to harmonize financial sector standards and establish effective consolidated supervision. Considering the serious damage to investor confidence caused by the crisis, it is widely expected that investors and lenders will place even greater emphasis on high-quality financial reporting. One of the key proposals arising from the April 2009 G-20 summit in London was to promote international financial stability through information exchange and international cooperation in financial supervision and surveillance. As more lessons from the financial crisis become clear, it is very likely that international standards will be further improved and fine-tuned. The World Bank provides a voice for its partner countries in such international forums, and it works to increase LAC and other developing countries' contributions to setting the standards.

Since the ROSC A&A program was initiated in 2001, the world has made much progress toward common international standards of financial transparency, accountability, and governance. The LAC region has not been at the leading edge of this movement, but there have been success stories and signs of growing momentum for reform. These trends are encouraging for everyone concerned with financial stability and the private sector–led growth that strong A&A standards are meant to promote. The authors of this book hope for continued and accelerated progress along this road in the coming years.

CHAPTER 1

Introduction and Background

In the Latin America and Caribbean (LAC) region, as in the rest of the world, reliable financial information is the cornerstone of a robust market economy and efficient public sector. Managers need reliable information about their companies' finances to make business decisions; lenders, to decide whether to make a loan; investors, to decide whether they should buy bonds or stock in a company; and regulators, to ensure that regulated entities live up to their obligations. Likewise, in the public sector, policy makers need to have reliable information to decide where to direct scarce resources, what investments to make, and whether public services are operating efficiently. Citizens and civil society require transparent information to make informed decisions about whether their tax or investment money is being spent responsibly, and to serve as a check on governments and businesses when needed. Thus, on an aggregate level, better information promotes development in the private and financial sectors, as well as accountability and efficiency in the public sector.

Underpinning a system of reliable financial information is a framework of sound accounting, auditing, and reporting practices. This framework is built with rigorous standards for accounting and auditing, skilled accountants and auditors, a satisfactory education system, and a robust enforcement regime.

The World Bank recognizes the importance of a strong accounting and auditing framework in the private and public sectors as part of a broad-based development strategy for LAC. Transparent and reliable financial information supports many of the LAC countries' development goals, such as access to finance for small and medium enterprises (SMEs), deepening of capital markets, an improved business climate for local and foreign businesses and investors, and sound management of state-owned enterprises (SOEs). The Bank assists partner countries by assessing the quality of their accounting and auditing frameworks and developing recommendations for reform through the Reports on the Observance of Standards and Codes (ROSCs) on Accounting and Auditing (A&A). In a number of countries, the Bank has also worked to mobilize funding to implement recommendations set out in ROSC A&A reports. It has also undertaken several other activities, particularly with regard to regional knowledge sharing, to support reforms proposed under the ROSC A&A. (An overview of the ROSC program is provided in appendixes A and B.)

This book presents both an analysis of the broader trends derived from the individual country-level studies produced under the ROSC A&A program and a synthesis of lessons learned from the Bank's experiences working with policy makers and other stakeholders to implement the ROSC A&A recommendations. This first chapter introduces the book by showing how sound A&A practices in the private and public sectors contribute to LAC's development agenda, and by describing the regional economic context. It then presents three case studies of successful financial reporting and auditing reforms within LAC, showing how these reforms have benefited the countries. It describes drivers of reform that have led some countries to adopt global standards of good A&A practice and others to take a more conservative, wait-and-see approach. Finally, the chapter describes the objectives and methodology of this study, and the structure of the book.

Importance of Accounting and Auditing for LAC's Economic Development

Sound accounting, auditing, and reporting practices are crucial for promoting sustainable and equitable private sector–led growth and strengthening governance and accountability.

Facilitating Access to Finance

Reliable financial reporting and auditing practices facilitate access to finance for local enterprises, particularly SMEs, and promote the development of capital markets. One significant impediment to private sector growth in the LAC region is the lack of financing available to companies at reasonable rates (Márquez, Barreix, and Villela 2007, 5).[1] Since financial markets in the region tend to be shallow, the overall funding available to the private sector is low (figure 1.1). Excluding Chile, which has the region's deepest financial sector, credit to the private sector amounts to just 24 percent of GDP (Andrade, Farrell, and Lund 2007). The lack of funding particularly hurts SMEs—the main providers of jobs in the region—because they are not large enough to raise capital abroad. Improved financial reporting by SMEs would increase their chances of borrowing at lower rates, as it would provide banks and venture capitalists access to standardized and reli-

Figure 1.1 A Comparative View of LAC's Financial Depth
Financial Assets as a Percentage of GDP, 2007 (Percent)

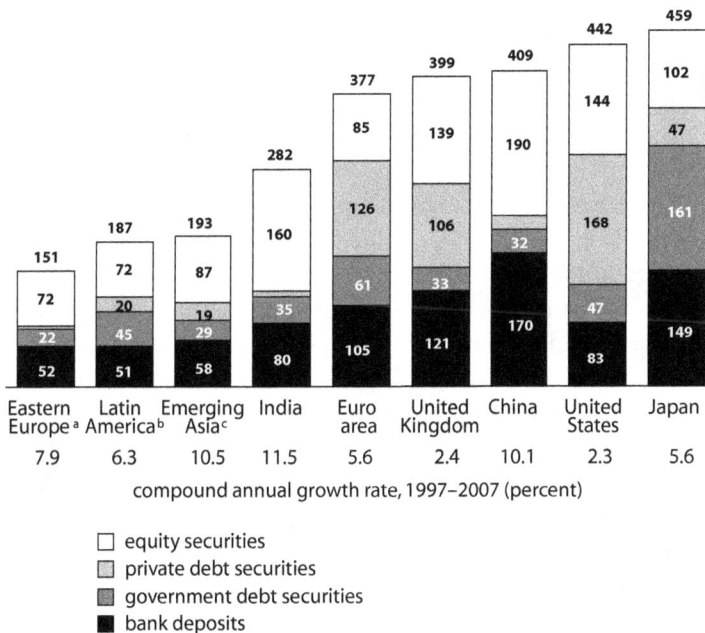

Eastern Europe[a]	Latin America[b]	Emerging Asia[c]	India	Euro area	United Kingdom	China	United States	Japan
7.9	6.3	10.5	11.5	5.6	2.4	10.1	2.3	5.6

compound annual growth rate, 1997–2007 (percent)

☐ equity securities
▨ private debt securities
▧ government debt securities
■ bank deposits

Source: McKinsey Global Institute Global Financial Asset database.

Note: Latest available data. Some figures may not sum to totals because of rounding.

a. Eastern Europe includes Croatia, the Czech Republic, Estonia, Hungary, Latvia, Lithuania, Poland, Romania, the Russian Federation, the Slovak Republic, Slovenia, Turkey, and Ukraine.

b. Latin America includes Argentina, Bolivia, Brazil, Chile, Colombia, Costa Rica, Ecuador, El Salvador, Guatemala, Honduras, Mexico, Panama, Peru, Uruguay, and República Bolivariana de Venezuela.

c. Emerging Asia includes Indonesia, Malaysia, the Philippines, the Republic of Korea, and Thailand.

able financial information (Rojas-Suarez 2007, 14). In addition, there is a dearth of long-term financing, since, with few exceptions (most notably Brazil and Chile), the region's capital markets remain underdeveloped and characterized by low liquidity (de la Torre, Gozzi, and Schmukler 2007a). If stock exchanges in the region are to increase listings and trading levels, they must enhance investor confidence; this will require, among other factors, the availability of complete and accurate financial information.

Promoting a Better Business Climate

A business climate that fosters investor confidence and attracts foreign and domestic investment requires sound practices of transparency, accountability, and governance—embodied in a financial reporting regime that provides investors, creditors, and other third parties with timely and accurate information for their investment and other business decisions. (Not only companies, but also governments benefit from such a regime: governments that follow good governance practices and are efficient in their public spending receive better ratings from the major credit rating agencies.) These considerations are especially significant for institutional investors, such as insurance companies and pension funds, which have fiduciary responsibility and are often prohibited from acquiring riskier securities rated below "investment grade."

Furthering Economic Integration

Financial reports that are comparable across countries are a boon to international investors and promote both deeper regional economic ties (for example, through the Dominican Republic–Central America Free Trade Agreement and the Caribbean Community) and economic integration with the rest of the world. Entrepreneurs in one country with aspirations to expand their businesses into neighboring countries frequently need to follow separate accounting standards for their businesses in different countries, and then to reconcile the disparate information in preparing consolidated financial statements. Adopting common financial reporting standards not only lowers the cost of doing businesses for these companies, but also facilitates cross-border investments, as potential investors can easily compare financial statements from other countries using standards they are familiar with (Hope, Jin, and Kang 2006; Covrig, Defond, and Hung 2007; Bradshaw, Bushee, and Miller 2004). Thus, adopting and applying internationally recognized rules and practices for business activities, especially standards relating to accounting and financial information, can deepen the integration and concomitant benefits of regional free-trade agreements. In addition, the application of international standards promotes greater integration of LAC economies on a global scale, particularly with the European Union and the United States, the region's main trading partners.

Effective Financial Oversight of SOEs

Sound financial reporting by SOEs allows for greater accountability and better allocation of capital, which in turn are important for increased efficiency in operations, better allocation of public sector resources, and more efficient investment in expanding and improving service delivery. Although many utilities and providers of essential services have been privatized in LAC, public enterprises continue to be significant economic players in the region. These public enterprises generally lack transparency and are often considered quite inefficient. This affects the economy and citizens significantly: financial losses in SOEs entail burdens for state treasuries and taxpayers, and they divert resources that could be used for other purposes. In some countries, these losses are large enough to jeopardize macroeconomic stability. In addition, chronic inefficiencies mean that citizens and local enterprises do not receive adequate basic services, which in the long run affects human development and private sector growth negatively. Finally, in countries that want to privatize their SOEs (wholly or in part), sound A&A practices facilitate the accurate valuation of companies, removing much uncertainty and probably resulting in more effective privatizations.

Financial Sector Stability: Accounting as an Essential Tool for Risk Monitoring and Mitigation

Accurate and timely financial information from banks, insurance companies, and pension funds allows for the more effective financial sector supervision that is required for financial sector stability and its related benefits, such as safeguarding savings and providing liquidity and investment capital to businesses. Financial institutions have diverse stakeholders whose interests are protected by a banking regulator: bank depositors want to know that their savings are protected, borrowers want assurance that the condition of their lender is sound and their loans will not be called prematurely, bank shareholders need to ensure that their ventures are not being mismanaged, and pension contributors want to make sure that their savings have been invested prudently. In addition, given that bank failures can occur quickly, on the basis of no more than rumor and innuendo, and that the failure of one bank can have a ripple effect on others, the public needs assurance about the health of the overall system.

LAC has seen its share of banking crises, and they have had substantial negative impacts: economic stagnation, strained public finances, and families driven into poverty. The most recent crisis—in the Dominican Republic, in early 2003—is estimated to have cost nearly 25 percent of the country's GDP (Laeven and Valencia 2008, 40). Moreover, financial institutions other than banks can generate significant systemic risk. As an element of fiduciary responsibility, banks, insurance companies, and pension funds should be held to good governance standards and required to produce regular, comprehensive, reliable, and transparent financial reports and to follow sound, reliable audit practices.

Accounting and Auditing in the LAC Regional Economic Context

Following decades of instability, the LAC region is now more economically and politically stable. Thus, it is in a better position to focus on financial and private sector development, and efforts to reform corporate financial reporting and auditing have begun to yield benefits.

New Economic and Political Stability

The 1950s through the 1970s were notable in most of LAC for the protection of domestic industries under the Import Substitution Industrialization model of development. The weakness of this model was largely masked by the availability of relatively cheap credit from international banks and other lenders, which were flush with deposits from oil-producing countries. The abundance of credit, coupled with the need to keep country economies running during the external shocks of the oil crises of 1973–74 and 1979, led LAC governments to amass significant debt. Although growth rates were healthy throughout the region during the 1970s, most countries had not yet undergone the pro-market reforms that are necessary for private sector–led development; consequently, A&A reform was not on their agenda (Loayza, Fajnzylber, and Calderón 2004; Bernanke 2005).

Nor could policy makers or investors turn their attention to microeconomic issues such as reliable financial information during the 1980s. Beginning in 1982, a number of LAC countries defaulted or came close to defaulting on their debt obligations. The region came to be perceived as a risky place to invest, and credit dried up. Moreover, much of the region was beset by high inflation throughout the decade, and nearly all

LAC economies contracted. It was a tumultuous period politically as well, with a return to democracy in South America and civil war in Central America. In the Caribbean, many countries gained their independence during the late 1970s and early 1980s, a political change that brought its own economic challenges (Bernanke 2005; Devlin and Ffrench-Davis 1995). During this time, then, most of the region's countries were obliged to focus on more macrolevel issues, such as controlling inflation, promoting rule of law, safeguarding against banking crises, or avoiding rapid currency devaluation. Governments, donors, civil society groups, and the private sector could not afford to focus their attention on the availability of reliable financial information.

Some of the problems of the 1980s lingered into the 1990s, but by the middle of the decade most countries had embarked on a reform path toward private sector–led growth (Loayza and Palacios 1997). The region has been able to reduce its external debt substantially since the 1990s. For instance, Brazil and Mexico have reduced their total external debt stocks to around 15 percent of gross national income. Nonetheless, a number of countries still face high levels of indebtedness—Jamaica's external debt represents 100 percent of gross national income, Uruguay's 54 percent, Argentina's 50 percent, and Chile's 40 percent (World Bank 2007).[2] (Table 1.1 provides an overview of the LAC economic context.)

Recent Developments

LAC has experienced relatively robust growth recently: its annual growth rate averaged approximately 5 percent in the last five years, fueled in part by significant institutional and policy improvements in macroeconomic and financial areas and a boom in international commodity prices. During this period, almost 60 million people were lifted out of poverty in the region (measured at US$4 a day, adjusted for purchasing power parity), and 41 million left the ranks of extreme poverty (measured at US$2 a day) (World Bank 2009b). However, the LAC region has historically been one of marked social and economic inequality, and although its social indicators have improved significantly during the last decade, it still lags considerably behind other emerging regions. For instance, infant mortality is higher, educational achievement lower, basic infrastructure much less developed, and income distribution much more unequal in LAC than in East Asia and Eastern Europe.

The region's social gains and growth are threatened, at least in the short term, by the global financial and economic crisis. The sharp drop in

Table 1.1 LAC's Key Economic Indicators

Country	Population (million) (2007)	GDP (US$ billion) (2007)	GDP growth (%) (2003–07)	Foreign direct investment (% of GDP) (2003–07)	Stocks traded (% of GDP) (2007)	Market capitalization (% of GDP) (2007)
Brazil	191.6	1,313.4	3.4	2.0	45.0	104
Mexico	105.3	1,022.8	3.3	2.6	11.0	39
Central America						
Belize	0.3	1.3	5.7	6.7	n.a.	n.a.
Costa Rica	4.5	26.3	6.2	4.6	0.0	8
El Salvador	6.9	20.4	2.9	2.0	0.0	33
Guatemala	13.4	33.9	3.1	0.7	—	—
Honduras	7.1	12.2	4.7	4.1	—	—
Nicaragua	5.6	5.7	4.0	5.2	—	—
Panama	3.3	19.5	6.7	8.7	1.0	32
Caribbean						
The Bahamas	0.3	6.6	1.2	3.5	—	—
Barbados	0.3	3.0	3.8	1.3	3.0	181
Dominican Republic	9.7	36.7	5.0	4.0	—	—
Eastern Caribbean	0.1	0.7	5.7	15.9	0.0	83
Guyana	0.7	1.1	1.2	7.1	0.0	24
Haiti	9.6	6.7	0.2	1.1	n.a.	n.a.
Jamaica	2.7	11.4	2.0	7.8	3.0	108
Suriname	0.5	2.2	6.3	—	—	—
Trinidad and Tobago	1.3	20.9	10.7	7.3	2.0	75
Andean						
Bolivia	9.5	13.1	4.9	1.0	—	17
Colombia	44.0	207.8	5.1	4.2	5.0	49
Ecuador	13.3	44.5	5.4	3.5	1.0	10
Peru	27.9	107.3	5.8	2.9	7.0	99
Venezuela, R. B. de	27.0	228.1	7.8	1.3	—	—
Southern Cone						
Argentina	39.5	262.5	8.9	2.3	3.0	33
Chile	16.6	163.9	4.9	6.1	27.0	130
Paraguay	6.1	12.2	3.8	1.0	—	—
Uruguay	3.3	23.1	6.9	4.6	0.0	1
LAC	**550.5**	**3,607.3**	**4.8**	**4.3**	**6.4**	**57**

Source: World Development Indicators 2009, except Trinidad and Tobago, Suriname, República Bolivariana de Venezuela, and Uruguay (population data from 2006); Barbados data only available up to 2005.

Note: n.a. = Not applicable. — = Not available.

commodity prices and oil prices during the last quarter of 2008 and the dramatic slowdown in world trade have already affected the region's economies.[3] An additional factor is LAC's dependence on remittances (particularly from the United States): in eight LAC countries, remittances represent more than 10 percent of GDP (World Bank 2008).[4] Although growth forecasts vary widely in this environment of economic uncertainty, the World Bank projects that, following a gain of 4.3 percent in 2008, LAC's economies will contract by 2.2 percent collectively in 2009 (World Bank 2009a).

Entrenched Interests Have Slowed Reform

Even with many of the pieces of the macroeconomic puzzle in place, many LAC countries have been slow to engage in modernizing their financial reporting and auditing frameworks. Part of the explanation lies in the fact that these reforms necessarily involve the contribution of a broad range of stakeholders—from the private sector (including SMEs and large regional corporations) to the public sector (including legislators and regulators) to academia.

Resistance to change is, of course, not unique to LAC, although some have argued that "corporatism"—the dominance of a few well-organized and wealthy interests—is particularly prevalent there (Ottaway 2001). In some LAC countries, resistance to change in A&A standards has been strong among large, closely held, family-run enterprises, which may prefer the ambiguity and relative opacity that the existing financial reporting frameworks afford them. Elsewhere, a powerful public university may resist efforts to modernize its accounting curriculum, or to implement an internationally recognized accounting certification, which would take away some of the value of the accounting degree it confers. The accounting profession itself has frequently resisted efforts to impose additional obligations upon its members. Finally, public servants may resist accepting international standards that were written in London or New York, which may not easily accommodate local circumstances or differences in their countries.

International Momentum for Reform

Adopting high-quality, internationally recognized financial reporting and auditing standards is a difficult task, in large part because these standards are more of a moving target than a fixed goal: there have been significant changes during the last decade in the standards and codes that underpin the international financial architecture. Especially since the corporate accounting scandals of the early 2000s (mainly in the United States and Europe—for example, Enron, Royal Ahold, Worldcom, and Parmalat), this moving target has been moving faster. Moreover, while there are a handful of Latin American representatives on the key standard-setting bodies, the design of reforms has usually been led by lawmakers in Europe or the United States. Consequently, LAC leaders find themselves being asked to undertake sometimes costly A&A reforms spawned by crises that occurred outside of their own countries. Given the fact that frequently there is debate even among the original adopters of these reforms,[5] it is understandable that some LAC policy makers have adopted a wait-and-see approach to financial reporting and auditing reforms. Nevertheless, most countries in the region are pressing forward with the reform agenda.

One major area of reform at the international level has been the establishment of independent audit oversight bodies. Responding to the accounting and auditing scandals, governments around the world—beginning with the United States (through the Sarbanes-Oxley Act of 2002) and the European Union (through the new Eighth Company Law Directive)—recognized that the audit profession's system of self-regulation was no longer sustainable. To restore the credibility of the audit profession, they instituted independent public oversight of it. These changes have since been adopted in many countries around the world.

Another crucial development is that International Financial Reporting Standards (IFRS) have finally emerged as the global standard for listed companies. The European Union required listed companies to use IFRS for their consolidated financial statements beginning in 2005. In 2005, nearly 7,000 listed companies in 25 countries were using IFRS; by 2007, more than 100 countries had adopted them. In 2006, the International Accounting Standards Board (IASB) and the U.S. Financial Accounting Standards Board issued a roadmap for convergence between IFRS and U.S. Generally Accepted Accounting Principles (U.S. GAAP) (IASB 2006). Then, in 2008, the U.S. Securities and Exchange Commission (SEC) issued its "Roadmap for the Potential Use of Financial Statements Prepared in Accordance with International Financial Reporting Standards by U.S. Issuers" for comment. This roadmap sets out several milestones that could lead to requiring the use of IFRS by U.S. securities issuers in 2014 (U.S. SEC 2008). Several countries in the LAC region have adopted IFRS for particular sectors: as of 2010, Brazil will require the adoption of IFRS for listed companies, banks, and insurance companies; Mexico for nonbank listed companies; and Chile for listed companies.

Reforming A&A in LAC: Three Success Stories

The region's recent focus on strengthening its corporate financial reporting framework has already begun to bear fruit—as the experiences of Brazil, Mexico, and Chile show.

Brazil's Novo Mercado Introduces Enhanced Financial Reporting Standards

Brazil is attracting overseas investors by playing their game. The Novo Mercado, a new stock market whose corporate governance rules mirror those of the United States and Europe, almost doubled its listings in 2006. And an index of companies that follow the regulations has outperformed the benchmark Bovespa index in the past 12 months.

"It went from water to wine," said Wagner Pinheiro, president of Petros, a pension fund. He said he had doubled his stock holdings over the past four years.

—International Herald Tribune, March 8, 2007

In 2000, the São Paulo Stock Exchange (BOVESPA)[6] surveyed stakeholders and found that (a) international and domestic investors were willing to provide investment capital to Brazilian companies, provided they could be assured that the rights of minority shareholders would be respected; and (b) Brazilian companies were willing to observe higher standards of governance if they could raise adequate amounts of investment capital at costs comparable to what was available on other major financial markets (Santana et al. 2008).

In response, BOVESPA launched three special listing segments requiring higher corporate governance standards—the Novo Mercado and two transitional levels—whose requirements are equivalent to those applicable on other major exchanges in the United States and Europe.[7] Among the requirements related to disclosure were that the accounting practices of firms listed on the Novo Mercado and the two transitional levels needed to follow IFRS or U.S. GAAP, and all listed firms would need to have their accounts audited.

Almost immediately, the Novo Mercado's higher standards of financial reporting and governance captured significant investor interest. Since

2001, an index of companies listed on the Novo Mercado and Levels 1 and 2 has outperformed the BOVESPA index by approximately 3 percent each year.[8] As of April 2009, 99 companies were listed on the Novo Mercado, 18 in Level 2, and 40 in Level 1; these companies accounted for 59.2 percent of market capitalization on all Brazilian markets. In October 2007, the stock exchange itself went public; its market capitalization became the largest among all emerging market countries. Foreign investors have purchased 74 percent of shares in new listings (Santana et al. 2008).

The Novo Mercado has been a successful experiment in market-driven, voluntary adoption of higher standards of corporate governance and financial transparency. Brazilian law does not require companies to follow these higher standards, but those that have chosen to follow them by listing on the Novo Mercado have benefited from increased investor interest and thus a lower cost of capital.

Mexico's Certified Public Accountant Designation

The renewal of the Professional Mutual Recognition Agreement motivates us to keep working to maintain the Mexican accounting profession at a world-class level; however, it implies a commitment to represent Mexico well in this important process of globalization.

—Jaime Sánchez-Mejorada Fernández
Chairman, Mexican Institute of Public Accountants (2007–08)

During the last decade, Mexico has created a cadre of professional accountants of internationally recognized quality, as embodied in the Contador Público Certificado (Certified Public Accountant, or CPC) designation. The more demanding requirements to obtain and maintain the CPC designation contribute to a better-qualified accounting profession and help to instill greater user confidence in the financial statements that these accountants prepare and audit. The CPC designation is considered equivalent to the U.S. and Canadian licenses, according to the Professional Mutual Recognition Agreement signed in 2002 pursuant to the North American Free Trade Agreement (Peek et al. 2007); thus, Mexican accountants who obtain the CPC credential may practice accountancy in the United States and Canada, after passing an exam on national standards and tax legislation.

The CPC designation brings several benefits for Mexico, its accounting profession, and its business environment. The years-long process of strengthening the credential generated efforts to create a standardized (and upgraded) accounting curriculum for Mexico's universities, thus strengthening the overall quality of the Mexican accounting profession (Peek et al. 2007). The international recognition brought added prestige to the Mexican accounting profession; over the long run, this should attract more qualified individuals to the profession. Furthermore, the supervisors of financial institutions and listed companies recognized the added rigor of the CPC designation and required that external auditors of supervised entities be CPCs. Thus, the introduction of the CPC designation generated a pool of qualified accountants who could be relied upon to audit the businesses whose financial health is a matter of public interest. In addition, the fact that the Mexican CPC designation is equivalent to U.S. and Canadian licenses provides added reassurance of the quality of the Mexican accounting profession to international investors who rely on Mexican companies' financial statements, facilitating cross-border investment.

Chile's Securities Market on Course toward IFRS Implementation

> The path that we have chosen is to trade a static view for a dynamic one, which helps mitigate the moral hazard of information asymmetries but at the same time demands greater flexibility and efficiency.
>
> —Guillermo Larraín, Chairman,
> Superintendency of Securities and Insurance, Chile

IFRS adoption is a serious and complex process, and Chile's experience serves as a useful model for other countries in the region. Its transition experience is particularly interesting because of the significance of its stock market (US$220 billion market capitalization in February 2008).

In October 2006, Chile's Superintendency of Securities and Insurance (Superintendencia de Valores y Seguros, or SVS) decided to require companies that are listed on its stock market and have a free float of more than 25 percent to publish IFRS financial statements for reporting periods starting on or after January 1, 2009. All other listed companies are to publish IFRS financial statements beginning in 2010. Chile was the first large country in the LAC region to adopt IFRS in full.

Since formally issuing the requirement to adopt IFRS, SVS has maintained a thorough engagement with various stakeholders to make the conversion process a success. This has entailed regular outreach to the business community; substantial training of its own staff as well as market participants; ongoing and transparent communication to ensure that the requirements and the time frame are properly understood and can be met; and close monitoring of companies' progress in preparing for implementation.

Chile's authorities have been very deliberate and careful about the switch to IFRS. Their efforts toward a smooth transition appear to be meeting with success, even though the change-over is taking place in the middle of the worst financial crisis in a generation.

Drivers of Reform in LAC Accounting and Auditing

External events and internal policy choices have led some LAC countries to move further along the path of reform than others. It is worthwhile to examine briefly some of the "drivers of reform" that have led some countries to adopt (or adapt) international standards of good practice in the realm of financial reporting and auditing policy.

External drivers of reform sometimes take the form of calamitous financial disruptions—such as a bank failure or the unexpected bankruptcy of a large, publicly traded company—that capture the public's attention and create political momentum for new regulations. During the 1990s, in particular, the LAC region saw a significant number of banking crises (Laeven and Valencia 2008) and high-profile corporate failures involving fraud.[9]

A second potential external driver of reform is a treaty obligation as part of a regional integration pact. For example, the North American Free Trade Agreement contained an article obligating the signatories to work toward mutual recognition of professional licenses and certifications. There is nearly identical language in the Dominican Republic–Central America Free Trade Agreement among Costa Rica, the Dominican Republic, El Salvador, Guatemala, Honduras, Nicaragua, and the United States (Peek et al. 2007).

A third driver of reform is the influence of a critical mass of large companies that are already complying with more rigorous standards of financial reporting and corporate governance by listing on European or U.S. stock exchanges. A case could be made that such large companies in Brazil and Chile helped to influence stock market regulators there to modify their standards to more closely match those of their North American and European counterparts.

As LAC's capital markets deepen, LAC countries must continue to improve their corporate financial reporting regimes to afford investors the same level of protection they enjoy on the major markets worldwide. Compared with industrial nations and with countries in the East Asia and Pacific region, LAC's markets are still relatively underdeveloped overall. Some markets (for example, Argentina and Panama) have shrunk as a result of delistings, while in most countries the market remains relatively narrow and shallow. However, LAC's capital markets have enjoyed significant relative growth over the last two decades, with stock market capitalization rising from 12.5 percent of GDP in 1990 to 42 percent in 2004 (de la Torre and Schmukler 2007, 46). In fact, capital market growth has been the main driver of overall financial sector growth in LAC for the period 2002–07, which showed an average 17.8 percent increase in bank deposits as compared with a 32.8 percent increase in equity securities (figure 1.2) (Andrade, Farrell, and Lund 2007).[10] Moreover, BM&F BOVESPA has become one of the leading exchanges of the world: 3 of the top 20 initial public offerings in 2007 involved Brazilian issuers and took place on BOVESPA (Ernst & Young 2008).[11] Chile's securities market has the highest ratio of market capitalization to GDP in the region (125 percent, which is similar to the U.S. ratio), thanks not only to the relatively high level of development the country has achieved, but also to a series of ambitious and successfully implemented capital market reforms. The significant growth of the region's capital markets has resulted in increased demand for high-quality financial information from listed companies. Since these growth trends are likely to continue, so will the demand for high-quality financial information.

The introduction of private pension funds is widely viewed as a primary factor behind the development of LAC's stock markets (García Herrero et al. 2002; de la Torre, Gozzi, and Schmukler 2007b). Over the past two decades, 12 Latin American countries have reformed their national retirement plans by shifting most pensions from social to individual responsibility. These governments have downsized the public pay-as-you-go component and introduced private schemes, such as mandatory individual private savings accounts and voluntary private pension plans. Chile was at the forefront of these reforms in the region when it introduced individual retirement accounts in 1981; other countries followed suit in the early 1990s. This shift has driven some national authorities to push for stronger standards of financial reporting and audit in listed companies, as retirement savings may be invested with these companies (de la Torre, Gozzi, and Schmukler 2007b).

In some countries (for example, Haiti, Panama, and Paraguay), in an effort to fight informality and impose a universally accepted high-quality

Figure 1.2 Latin America's Deepening Financial Markets
Total Financial Assets for Latin America (US$ billions)

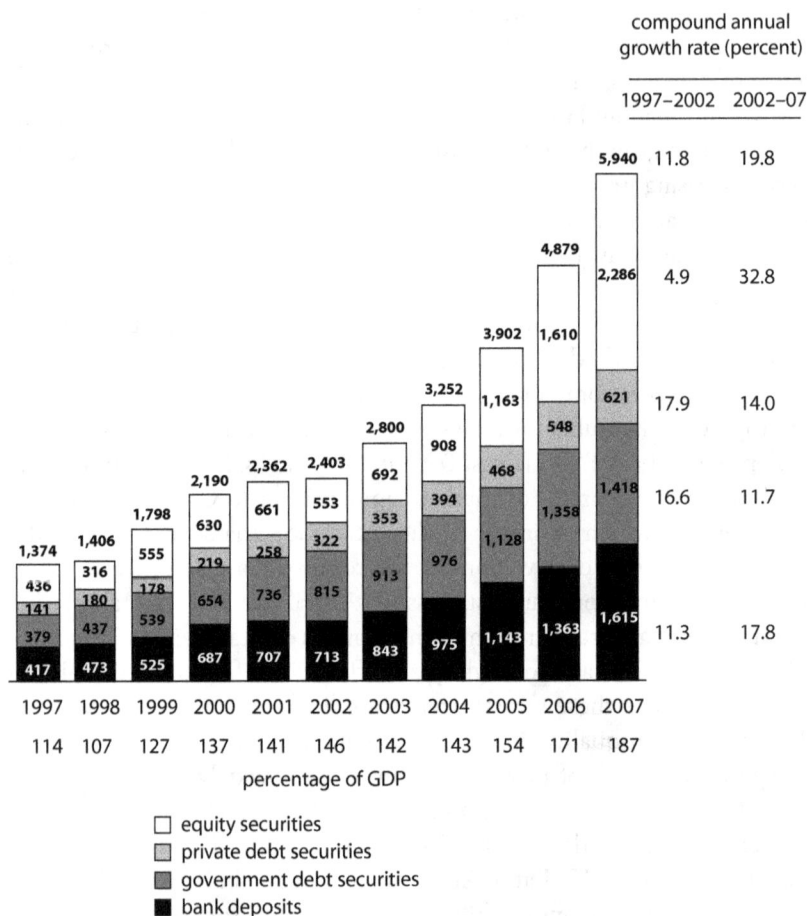

	compound annual growth rate (percent)	
	1997–2002	2002–07
5,940	11.8	19.8
2,286	4.9	32.8
621	17.9	14.0
1,418	16.6	11.7
1,615	11.3	17.8

Bar chart data:

Year	Total	equity securities	private debt securities	government debt securities	bank deposits
1997	1,374	141	436	379	417
1998	1,406	180	316	437	473
1999	1,798	178	555	539	525
2000	2,190	219	630	654	687
2001	2,362	258	661	736	707
2002	2,403	322	553	815	713
2003	2,800	353	692	913	843
2004	3,252	394	908	976	975
2005	3,902	468	1,163	1,128	1,143
2006	4,879	548	1,610	1,358	1,363
2007	5,940	621	2,286	1,418	1,615

percentage of GDP

1997	1998	1999	2000	2001	2002	2003	2004	2005	2006	2007
114	107	127	137	141	146	142	143	154	171	187

☐ equity securities
☐ private debt securities
☐ government debt securities
■ bank deposits

Source: McKinsey Global Institute Global Financial Asset database.

Note: At constant 2007 dollars and exchange rates. Includes Argentina, Bolivia, Brazil, Chile, Colombia, Costa Rica, Ecuador, El Salvador, Guatemala, Honduras, Mexico, Panama, Peru, Uruguay, and República Bolivariana de Venezuela.

financial reporting standard, the tax administration has required companies to follow heightened financial reporting and auditing requirements
for tax-reporting purposes. Although IFRS were not designed for tax-
reporting purposes, the adoption of a more rigorous financial reporting
standard can be a major improvement over what came before it.

The economic crisis that began in 2008 in the United States is likely to lead to calls for reform in LAC. Because of the crisis, the U.S. economy contracted 3.2 percent and the Euro Area economies contracted 4.1 percent during the fourth quarter of 2008 and the first quarter of 2009 (Eurostat 2009). One survey estimated that the world's high-net-worth individuals have lost a combined US$10 trillion of wealth because of the crisis (*Economist* 2009). In the aftermath of the crisis, significant regulatory changes are likely. The role played by major international credit rating agencies that gave top ratings to mortgage-backed securities, credit-default swaps, and other complex financial products—as well as that of the companies that dealt in them—is likely to draw considerable scrutiny (Geithner and Summers 2009). Some critics have focused on the fact that a number of U.S. regulatory agencies were responsible for overseeing various segments of the financial sector, but none was responsible for monitoring overall systemic risk. Some have even suggested the idea of a global systemic risk regulator (Rogoff 2009). Furthermore, the well-publicized Madoff and Stanford fraud cases have raised questions about auditor oversight requirements for wealth-management firms, as both Madoff and Stanford employed small, unknown audit firms to sign off on their financial statements. Even as this book is being finalized, A&A issues have returned to the front pages: public debates are still under way on the merits of "mark-to-market" and fair value accounting and a perceived lack of transparency surrounding many of the exotic financial products that helped to precipitate the crisis. It remains to be seen what reforms will arise from this global financial crisis. But whatever the shape and extent of the ultimate regulatory reforms, these changes are likely to be reflected in international standards, and there will be calls for the regulatory entities and other policy makers in the LAC region to implement analogous changes in their countries.

These are just a few examples of external and internal drivers that lead policy makers to push forward with reforms, but there are many reasons for pursuing an agenda of sound financial reporting and auditing standards. Together, the drivers of change offer an opportunity for LAC policy makers to narrow the remaining gap between national standards and international standards of good practice. This book aims to put policy makers and active members of the accounting profession in the driver's seat—to give them the tools to proactively pursue good-practice policies rather than merely react to unfavorable events as they occur.

About This Book

Eight years after the launch of the ROSC A&A program in LAC, A&A assessments have been completed for most of the countries in the region. This book is designed to synthesize the knowledge that has been acquired and published through this initiative.

Objectives

The purpose of this book is twofold. First, it is an analytic document—an attempt to summarize the lessons learned from conducting ROSC A&A in the region. It (a) analyzes the country-level data and draws cross-country conclusions, thus enabling policy makers and stakeholders to compare their country's performance with that of other countries in the region; (b) identifies the key characteristics of successful A&A reform initiatives, as well as the main obstacles to reform; and (c) highlights replicable solutions or potential areas for collaboration. Second, the book is a knowledge product, designed to inform the policy dialogue by raising awareness of A&A issues among government officials, the accounting profession, the private sector, academia, and civil society in LAC countries. It also seeks to disseminate the lessons learned to key players at the international and regional levels, including the donor community, to generate momentum for A&A reform throughout the region.

The study is based on desk reviews of the 17 ROSC A&A reports completed in the LAC region, a review of outside literature, and World Bank experience in engaging regional and international policy makers in dialogue on the issues raised in the ROSCs and in designing and implementing technical assistance projects and other initiatives to promote the implementation of the ROSCs' recommendations (see box 1.1).

It is important to note that the LAC region is not a monolith. While LAC countries share many characteristics and are bound by geography, there are important differences in languages, culture, and history. For instance, the English-speaking Caribbean states gained their independence relatively recently. Even within the Caribbean, countries like the Dominican Republic, Haiti, and Jamaica share similar geographic characteristics but speak different languages, have different legal traditions, and are at different stages of economic development. A large country like Brazil is dissimilar in many respects to a much smaller and poorer country like Nicaragua. To some extent, LAC can be seen as comprising several subregions—Mexico, Central America, the Caribbean, the Andean countries, Brazil, and the Southern Cone. However, an analysis of the ROSC A&A studies for most of the countries of the region reveals that

Box 1.1

ROSC A&A Follow-Up Activities

The World Bank carries out follow-up activities to assist countries in developing their A&A standards and practices. The Bank's experience in implementing these activities also informs the conclusions drawn in this report, especially in chapter 7. In LAC, ROSC-related activities have included the following:

- Several technical assistance projects (for example, a project funded by the UK Department for International Development in five Central American countries that focused on accounting education at the tertiary level, the development of a private-sector A&A country action plan in Peru, and a project to assist Honduran authorities in strengthening the country's institutional framework for A&A)
- "Virtual" seminars, in which participants from a number of countries in the region are brought together via satellite connection to discuss relevant issues (for example, IFRS for SMEs, insurance accounting, public oversight of the audit profession)
- The annual CReCER Regional Conference[a] on Accounting and Accountability for Regional Economic Growth, which brings together several hundred participants from the public and private sectors, the accounting profession, and academia.

a. More information on the CReCER Regional Conference is available at www.creceramericas.org.

the challenges LAC's policy makers face in crafting sound A&A frameworks have more elements in common than might be expected. Even though a region-wide study necessarily involves a certain degree of simplification, the authors have sought to avoid over-simplification by reflecting relevant circumstances of a country or subregional group.

Structure
The remainder of the book is structured similarly to a ROSC A&A report: chapters 2 through 6 summarize the main findings of the reports by topic.

- *The statutory framework (chapter 2).* The statutory framework is the set of rules (laws, decrees, regulations, standards, and so forth) that companies must follow with regard to accounting, auditing, and reporting. A statutory framework that is demanding, yet in line with a country's business needs and capacity level (that is companies' ability to comply and regulators' capacity to enforce), sets the stage for a robust A&A system. This chapter assesses the statutory frameworks of LAC countries with regard to their completeness, coherence, adaptability, and differentiation.

- *The accounting and auditing profession (chapter 3).* The effectiveness of A&A rules and standards depends in part on the capabilities and competence of those who are to apply them—mainly accountants and auditors. This chapter evaluates the institutions charged with the organization and oversight of A&A professionals, describes the necessary qualifications to practice as an accountant or auditor, and assesses how well the profession performs its functions.
- *Accounting education (chapter 4).* A strong education system is the foundation of a well-trained accounting and audit profession. This chapter, which looks at accounting education at the tertiary level in LAC, is based primarily on the preliminary findings of a study on accounting education in Latin America, commissioned in connection with the ROSC A&A Program for LAC.
- *The accounting and auditing standards and standard-setting process (chapter 5).* One of the most important global trends in corporate financial reporting is the gradual move toward the adoption of international A&A standards. This chapter describes the existing A&A standards in LAC, these countries' progress toward adopting international standards, and the processes for setting new A&A standards.
- *Enforcement of accounting and auditing standards (chapter 6).* Each LAC country has a number of regulatory authorities that are charged with enforcing compliance with applicable A&A standards. These regulators play a critical role in ensuring well-functioning, stable financial sectors and markets. This chapter considers the institutions and processes used to enforce auditing standards in the LAC region.

Finally, chapter 7 identifies priority areas of focus for future reforms within the three pillars of sound financial reporting systems. None of the highlighted priority reforms is easy, but the authors consider that these are the reforms toward which policy makers should direct their energies to achieve greatest impact with their limited resources.

The authors believe this book will provide a useful synthesis of the knowledge that has been acquired and published through the ROSC

A&A initiative. A&A remains an important concern for policy makers and the donor community, and the authors hope this publication not only captures the state of the A&A environment in LAC today, but also provokes a continued dialogue to help the region's leaders and policy makers push forward with financial reporting reforms over the next several years.

Notes

1. Because of varying definitions of the term and a high degree of informality, concrete statistics for Latin American SMEs are difficult to find, but one Inter-American Development Bank study estimates that 80 percent of employment in the region is generated by microenterprises and SMEs (Márquez, Barreix, and Villela 2007).

2. According to Economist Intelligence Unit data, the comparable figures for total external debt stocks in 2007, expressed as a percentage of gross domestic product, are: Brazil: 17.2 percent; Mexico: 17.5 percent; Jamaica: 74.9 percent; Uruguay: 45.6 percent; Argentina: 51.8 percent; and Chile: 34.6 percent.

3. Economist Intelligence Unit quarterly data for "world commodity forecasts" and crude oil.

4. 25 percent for Honduras, 22 percent for Guyana and Haiti, and 18 percent for El Salvador and Jamaica (data for 2006).

5. For instance, on May 18, 2009, the U.S. Supreme Court agreed to hear a case alleging that the Public Companies Accounting Oversight Board (PCAOB) created by the Sarbanes-Oxley Act is unconstitutional because it is too independent from executive and legislative oversight. This independence from political influence is a key feature of the accounting oversight board's design.

6. In May 2008, BOVESPA merged with the Brazilian Mercantile and Futures Exchange to form a new company called BM&F BOVESPA: Brazil's Securities, Commodities, and Futures Exchange.

7. BOVESPA also created transitional Levels (1 and 2) as stepping stones for companies wishing to become listed on the Novo Mercado, but that cannot comply with or have concerns about its full governance requirements. Level 1 requirements are similar to traditional Brazilian regulations but establish additional obligations related to disclosure of information. Level 2 requires that companies comply with almost all obligations of the Novo Mercado, except that they may retain their preferred shares.

8. From 2001 (the first full year of the Novo Mercado's operation) to April 2009, shares in the "Corporate Governance Index"—including companies from Novo Mercado and Levels 1 and 2—have risen by an average of 2.97

percent more per year than the Bovespa Index. (http://www.bovespa .com.br).

9. The ROSC A&A for Chile cites the Inverlink company's bankruptcy, and the (forthcoming) Panama ROSC A&A cites the ADELAG Group's failure. These are mentioned here merely as illustrative examples.

10. Much of this is due to foreign investors, who injected US$12 billion in new money into Latin American equity markets in 2005 (Andrade, Farrell, and Lund 2007).

11. BM&F BOVESPA's equity domestic market capitalization was US$592 at the end of 2008, which was more than, for instance, those of Italy's or South Africa's exchanges (World Federation of Exchanges, http://www.world-exchange.org).

CHAPTER 2

National Corporate Financial Reporting Frameworks

Bringing the Pieces Together in a Fragmented Landscape

The statutory frameworks of Latin American and Caribbean (LAC) countries vary significantly in terms of accounting, auditing, and reporting requirements for the corporate sector. Most LAC countries follow a civil law legal system, although those with a history as British territories or colonies (Belize, Guyana, Jamaica, Trinidad and Tobago, and the nine members of the Organization of Eastern Caribbean States) have a common law system. But even among countries that share a legal tradition, the accounting and auditing (A&A) requirements have evolved differently in response to varying business needs and the financial and economic environment. For example, faced with economic travails and upswings, some countries have deregulated and some have added more regulations. Moreover, in some countries the authors of legislation and regulation are quite savvy about corporate financial reporting, while in others there is a lack of corporate financial experience and skills at both the policy-making and regulatory levels. The result is significant diversity in the laws that govern corporations, government regulators, and other economic actors in the region.

This section focuses on the statutory framework for corporate financial reporting, which comprises all laws, regulations, and other rules pertaining to accounting, auditing, and financial reporting that companies are obliged to follow. The company laws and accompanying regulations provide the overall shape of the A&A environment. Subsequent regulations, resolutions, and policy circulars can fill in crucial details. A strong corporate financial reporting framework is an important first step to an enhanced business environment.

This study evaluates countries' statutory frameworks for A&A as measured by four main attributes: completeness, coherence, adaptability, and degree of differentiation.[1] *Completeness* means that the law contains all the requirements of a financial reporting regime and establishes institutions that are empowered to enforce and capable of enforcing those requirements. *Coherence* means that the body of laws does not contain internal contradictions with regard to the authority of various branches of the state (tax authorities, financial sector regulators, and others), and that the laws do not overlap in a way that may generate confusion about the exact legal requirements for particular entities. *Adaptability* means that the law does not contain requirements that are necessarily subject to change over time (for example, international accounting standards of a particular year, or specific fines for infractions). Finally, a *differentiated* A&A statutory framework makes a clear distinction between public interest entities (PIEs; see box 2.1) and enterprises that do not serve the public interest, including most small and medium enterprises (SMEs); PIEs merit greater regulatory oversight than non-PIEs.

Completeness

The law should require that each year PIEs produce a set of complete financial statements that include the documentation users need to ascertain the company's financial situation. At a minimum, a complete statutory framework includes the following provisions[2]:

- It requires PIEs to prepare four general-purpose financial statements—(a) a balance sheet, (b) an income statement, (c) a statement of cash flows, and (d) a statement of changes in shareholders' equity—and a complete set of accompanying notes setting out key accounting policies, appropriate explanations for important elements of the four finan-

Box 2.1

Public Interest Entities (PIEs)

There is no universally recognized definition of a PIE; this concept has emerged relatively recently, and countries may define the term differently depending on local realities. The International Accounting Standards Board described PIEs as entities that meet one or more of the following conditions:

- Receive funds from the public in a fiduciary capacity (that is, banks, savings and loan institutions, investment funds, pension funds, and insurance companies)
- Provide essential public services and are subject to public procurement
- Are active in strategic sectors in the economy, such as defense, or operate as monopolies
- Are owned by the state
- Have issued or have taken legal steps to issue securities on an exchange, or have a large number of shareholders representing a substantial ownership interest or
- Are economically significant to the country as a whole. Significance can be measured through such indicators as revenues, number of employees, and amount of assets.

cial statements, and other information necessary for a proper understanding of the financial statements.

- It requires PIEs to prepare consolidated financial statements for the whole economic group, in addition to the legal entity financial statements. Legal entity financial statements are important for dividend distribution, compliance with loan covenants, taxation, and other purposes. Investors and other general-purpose users normally rely more on consolidated financial statements for assessing the company's overall economic performance and financial situation.[3]
- It requires PIEs (or, at a minimum, supervised entities) to prepare a report, often referred to as a Management Discussion and Analysis (MD&A), that qualitatively describes the state of the enterprise, providing necessary contextual details that help users make sense of the financial data presented in the other statements.
- It requires that the financial statements of PIEs be audited annually and submitted to shareholders and other users soon after the relevant

reporting period ends. Financial information loses much of its value as
time passes, so timeliness in financial reporting is critical.
- It requires PIEs to have an audit committee as a part of a strong internal control and corporate governance system. Audit committee members should be competent in matters of financial reporting and auditing. It is desirable that a majority of them be independent from
management and controlling shareholders.
- It requires that PIEs' financial statements be published broadly—the
Internet allows low-cost publication on the company's and the relevant
regulatory body's Web site—or otherwise easily accessible to the
public.

Complete Financial Statements

LAC countries generally have a fairly complete statutory framework,
requiring the basic elements of a corporate financial reporting regime.
Every country surveyed as part of the Reports on the Observance of
Standards and Codes, Accounting and Auditing (ROSC A&A) requires a
balance sheet, an income statement, and explanatory notes from their
PIEs, and nearly all countries require a cash flow statement and a statement of changes in equity. However, a few require, instead of the cash
flow statement, a "statement of origins and applications of funds."
Investors and other users consider the usefulness of this statement to be
limited because it does not show the breakdown of cash flows by main
category of activities (operating, investing, and financing), which are key
indicators of financial performance and cannot be derived simply from
the other statements.

Consolidated Financial Statements

Most LAC countries also require PIEs to prepare consolidated financial
statements, in accordance with good international practice. The notable
exceptions are Brazil (which requires only listed companies to prepare
consolidated financial statements) and Colombia (which does not require
banks to consolidate the financial statements of non-bank subsidiaries,
and vice versa). It is good practice for an economic group to issue consolidated financial statements for the group and distinct sets of legal entity
financial statements for each of its segments. Consolidated financial statements are used for financial analysis and investment decisions, and legal
entity financial statements are used to calculate income taxes, dividends,
profit-sharing compliance with loan covenants, and prudential regulation.

Without consolidated financial statements, potential investors get, at best, an incomplete picture of the company. Nevertheless, it is considered good practice to exempt small economic entities from the requirement to consolidate their financial statements (IASB 2004).

In general, LAC country laws do not set specific requirements for consolidated financial statements. The silence of the law in this respect can be viewed as an opportunity for policy makers to gradually update their financial reporting rules for general-purpose financial statements. For example, by focusing only on consolidated financial statements, Brazil was able to align its gene∅ral-purpose financial reporting rules with international standards without needing to overhaul its regulatory framework. Changes in the requirements for consolidated financial statements did not affect Brazil's tax or prudential reporting requirements, which are based on legal entity financial statements. It has since required International Financial Reporting Standards (IFRS) for the consolidated financial statements of banks, listed companies, and insurance companies without modifying the requirements for legal entity financial statements.

Management Discussion and Analysis

A proper MD&A provides important qualitative, contextual information and analysis to accompany the quantitative data presented in the financial statements (Meiers 2006). Argentina, Brazil, Chile, Peru, and Uruguay require listed companies to produce an MD&A—a positive development.

Statutory Audits

All LAC countries require regulated PIEs to undergo an annual external audit of their financial statements (table 2.1). A few countries have arguably gone too far by requiring all companies, regardless of their size or their significance to the economy, to undergo a statutory audit. This universal requirement fails to differentiate between PIEs, which need more stringent oversight, and non-PIEs, which are hampered by excessive requirements.

Audit Committees and Other Internal Financial Oversight Agents

LAC countries often charge an individual or group with internal financial oversight functions that may duplicate the roles of the external auditor and audit committee. Good corporate governance requires that companies set up a body or designate an individual or a committee to interact

Table 2.1   Commercial Entities Subject to Statutory Audit
(State-owned enterprises excluded)

Country	PIEs	Large private companies	SMEs
Argentina	√	√	*
Brazil	√	√	
Chile	√		
Colombia	√	√	√
Dominican Republic	√	√	√
Ecuador	√	√	
El Salvador	√	√	√
Haiti	√	√	√
Honduras	√		
Jamaica	√	√	√
Mexico	√	√	
OECS	√	√	
Panama	√	√	√
Paraguay	√	√	
Peru	√		
Uruguay	√	√	

Source: LAC ROSC A&A review, http://www.worldbank.org/ifa/rosc_aa.html.

Note: OECS = Organisation of Eastern Caribbean States.

* All corporations (*Sociedad Anónima*, or SA) are required to be audited.

with the external auditor and serve as an independent safeguard of the company's financial reporting integrity and compliance (OECD 2008). In Latin America, nearly every country's company law designates a *comisario, síndico, revisor fiscal, conselho fiscal, or inspector de cuentas* (table 2.2), who must be retained from outside the company but whose responsibilities, training, and prior experience are not well defined. Some of these individuals may not be well equipped to perform an internal audit function. Moreover, in some cases the person is required to be a shareholder, which calls into question that person's independence and reliability.

There is a growing movement to require companies, particularly banks and other regulated entities, to establish audit committees. Audit committees are made up of independent members of a company's board of directors and are responsible to the board (and the public at large) for overseeing the quality of corporate financial reporting, including hiring and overseeing the external auditor and ensuring compliance with financial reporting requirements. Approximately half of the countries reviewed under the ROSC program in Latin America require their banks and other financial institutions to appoint an audit committee.

Table 2.2 Internal Control and Other Financial Oversight Mechanisms in PIEs

Country	Audit committee (or equivalent)	Comisario (or equivalent)	Comment
Argentina	√	√	*Comisión fiscalizadora* for regulated companies: a *síndico* for large, nonlisted companies.
Brazil	√		Audit committee for financial institutions and *conselho fiscal* for corporations (*conselho fiscal* is considered somewhat equivalent to an audit committee for those companies that are also listed on the New York Stock Exchange).
Chile	√		Banks have begun to introduce audit committees on a voluntary basis. Listed companies with a market value exceeding about $40 million must have a "directors' committee," somewhat equivalent to an audit committee.
Colombia		√	All companies are required to have a *revisor fiscal*, whose function is partly audit and partly internal control.
Dominican Republic		√	Code of Commerce requires the appointment of a *comisario*.
Ecuador		√	Financial institutions must appoint an internal auditor; corporations law requires the appointment of a *comisario*.
Honduras	√	√	All corporations must appoint a *comisario*; financial institutions must have an audit committee.
Mexico	√		Any company with more than 50 members (shareholders or guarantors), and all listed companies, must appoint an audit committee.
OECS	√		Financial institutions must appoint an audit committee, while audit committees are voluntary for listed companies.
Panama	√		Audit committee required for banks, voluntary for listed companies.
Paraguay	√	√	Audit committee required for financial institutions; *síndico* required for listed companies.
Uruguay	√	√	Banks must appoint an audit committee; listed companies must appoint a *síndico* or a *comisión fiscal*.

Source: LAC ROSC A&A review.

Note: OECS = Organisation of Eastern Caribbean States.

Public Disclosure of Financial Statements

Publication provides a useful disincentive for inaccuracies or outright deception in corporate financial statements. To quote the legal scholar and U.S. Supreme Court Justice Louis Brandeis, "Sunlight is the best disinfectant; electric light the best policeman." Transparency also provides the basis for third parties to exercise market discipline in extending loans or investing in a company.

While most countries require public financial disclosure from listed companies and other PIEs, there is a great deal of variation across countries regarding the legal requirements on the disclosure of financial statements of nonregulated companies. In the United Kingdom and Norway, for example, nearly all companies are required to disclose their financial statements, while in the Russian Federation and the United States there is no requirement for unregulated companies to disclose financial information publicly. The World Bank has no official policy position regarding the mandatory disclosure of financial statements for nonregulated companies. Nonetheless, the ROSC A&A often recommends public disclosure of all PIE financial statements to the extent that it is practicable through the Internet and can help foster a business climate conducive to private investment.

In the LAC countries surveyed under the ROSC program, banks, listed companies, and other PIEs are usually required to publish financial information, in line with good international practice (table 2.3). The Internet provides an inexpensive and broadly accessible means of disseminating financial information; thus, policy makers should move to require PIEs to publish their financial statements online. In a few cases, LAC companies are not required to publish the accompanying notes to their financial statements (for example, financial institutions in Colombia and insurance companies in the Dominican Republic or Uruguay)—a serious shortcoming, since the notes are an integral part of every financial statement and are necessary for understanding the company's financial position.

Coherence

The statutory framework needs to be clear enough for companies to follow. A coherent statutory framework has the following characteristics:

- It is not overly fragmented. The responsibility for regulating and enforcing A&A laws is not distributed across many different institutions,

Table 2.3 Requirements for the Public Disclosure of Financial Statements (in full)

Country	Banks	Insurance	Pension funds	Listed companies	Large nonlisted companies	SMEs	State-owned enterprises
Argentina	√	√	√	√	√	*	
Brazil	√	√	√	√	*	*	√
Chile	√	√	√	√	√		√
Colombia	√	√	√	√			√
Dominican Republic	√			√			
Ecuador	√	√	√				
El Salvador	√	√	√	√			
Haiti				n.a.			
Honduras	√	√	√	√.			√
Jamaica	√	√		√			
Mexico	√	√	√	√	√		
OECS	√			√			√
Panama	√		√	√			√
Paraguay	√	√	√	√			
Peru	√	√	√	√			
Uruguay	√	√	√	√	√		√

Source: LAC ROSC A&A review.

Note: n.a. = Not applicable; OECS = Organisation of Eastern Caribbean States.

* For corporations (*Sociedad Anónima*, or SA).

often with unclear or overlapping jurisdictions. Lawmakers should aim for fewer regulatory institutions, and clearly demarcate the boundaries of each institution's authority with respect to the others (Cihák and Podpiera 2006; Podpiera and Cihák 2007).

- It makes a clear separation between (a) tax, prudential, or other types of regulatory reporting and (b) general-purpose financial reporting. While sharing some common features, each type of reporting serves fundamentally different purposes.[4] Rather than imposing rules for general-purpose financial statements that adhere to a taxation or prudential focus, regulators should require *additional* or *separate* prudential information from companies (European Commission 1999, 2).[5]

Although LAC countries generally possess a complete statutory framework, the coherence of the framework is frequently not up to international good practice. LAC authorities (for example, sectoral regulators) and the accounting profession have often followed a piecemeal approach to issuing A&A regulations, creating duplication in certain areas and leaving gaps in others. In most countries there is no specific accounting law or audit law; corporate financial reporting requirements are often scattered among many different laws and regulations. Different financial reporting regimes tend to apply for banks, insurance companies, pension funds, state-owned enterprises (SOEs), and listed companies. In some cases, there may even be separate A&A standards for meatpacking companies, cooperatives, agro-companies, and offshore companies—all set by different regulators. This thicket of overlapping rules and accounting standards reduces transparency and makes it difficult, if not impossible, to compare and evaluate financial statements from companies across different sectors or internationally; and if multiple regulatory agencies are involved, the rules are harder to enforce. To reduce the likelihood of conflicting regulations, it is desirable for fewer institutions to have the power to issue financial reporting rules.

Another problem is that most LAC countries make no distinction between the prudential financial statements that supervised entities present to regulators and the general-purpose statements that potential investors or others would use to evaluate and compare companies. When there is a conflict between prudential rules and general-purpose rules, prudential rules usually take precedence. Given that every country's prudential accounting rules may entail slightly different valuation and recognition requirements, the lack of a clear distinction is a burden on users of financial information, who find it difficult to compare companies' performance with that of their peers in different countries or in different sectors of the economy. In some countries, the banking sector has tried to address this problem by including a note describing the differences between the accounting standards issued by the banking superintendent and IFRS. This guidance may aid potential investors by pointing to areas where prudential accounting requirements affect the financial statements. (This issue is further discussed in chapter 5.)

The influence of tax rules on general-purpose financial statements is a problem in many jurisdictions. In many cases accounting requirements have been established to enhance tax collection. Companies often prepare their general-purpose financial statements with the tax assessor in mind, especially where tax rules are not clearly separated from general-purpose accounting rules (Street 2003, 14).[6] In Brazil, for example, some companies reportedly refuse to use certain accepted accounting practices lest they trigger a tax assessment. In countries such as Honduras, Panama, and Paraguay, there is no legal differentiation between general-purpose financial reporting and tax reporting; where the recognition and valuation rules conflict, tax rules take legal precedence over the general-purpose accounting standard. Under these circumstances, companies have an incentive to understate their earnings and profits to minimize their tax burden, and the perception is that they do so. This perception alone, not to mention the actual practice of preparing misleading financial statements, reduces confidence in the reliability of these companies' financial statements.

Adaptability

The need to update financial reporting regimes continuously to reflect international standards and good practice calls for a measure of flexibility in the way the statutory framework is structured. Accordingly, it is preferable that the law enshrine only the core principles underpinning the A&A regime, leaving implementing regulations (including accounting standards) to be issued through separate instruments. A&A standards are constantly evolving,[7] and legislatures and lawmaking processes often move too slowly or are too politicized to keep up with necessary changes in A&A requirements. Governments that set their accounting standards in law (by mandating a specific version of IFRS, for example) risk having their accounting and business community fall behind the times. Thus, it is better practice to legislate only the basic framework, as described above. Rules that are likely to change in the short to medium term (for example, specific requirements to follow, the specific sanctions for not following them, and other enabling regulations) should be issued separately by the institutions that administer the laws. (This approach is discussed in greater detail in chapter 5.) Among the countries surveyed through the ROSC assessment, three—Brazil, Colombia, and the Dominican Republic—set a significant portion of their accounting standards into law but have taken steps to address this problem. The other countries surveyed enjoy a greater degree of legal flexibility.

Differentiation

Different types and sizes of companies demand different treatment under the law. Financial institutions, listed companies, and SOEs all have greater fiduciary responsibilities to depositors, shareholders, or the public at large than other closely held, nonfinancial companies. When dealing with corporate financial reporting issues, policy makers need to keep these distinctions in mind and tailor laws to fit the companies they regulate.

PIEs versus Non-PIEs

The law should clearly distinguish between PIEs and non-PIEs (comprising micro, small, and medium enterprises). A more limited regulatory regime should apply to non-PIEs (including a simpler set of accounting rules, elimination of the statutory audit requirement, and less frequent or no reporting). When smaller enterprises must follow the same stringent requirements as the largest companies, it needlessly increases the cost of doing business for those companies that comply with the law and degrades the rule of law among those companies that do not comply.

Most countries in LAC do not provide enough relief for micro, small, and medium enterprises. SMEs are the backbone of most LAC economies; the World Bank estimates that they provide approximately 95 percent of employment and nearly 70 percent of GDP in middle-income countries (Fan, Criscuolo, and Ilieva-Hamel 2005). It is important, then, that governments not hamper SMEs with unnecessary or unduly complex regulations. Most countries in the region have no specific standards for non-PIEs, but a few explicitly require them to follow the same standards as the largest PIEs (Uruguay, for example, requires all companies to follow IFRS). Furthermore, even if SMEs are required to apply IFRS under the law, in practice few of them do so—either because they are not capable of it or because it would be too costly to hire outside accountants with the necessary skills. A low level of compliance reduces the credibility of the companies and of the law that theoretically binds them, as most countries do not devote the necessary resources to enforcing these requirements (chapter 6). In this context, it is understandable that lenders and other users of financial statements have low confidence in the reliability and trustworthiness of unregulated companies' financial statements. (Box 2.2 describes an effort to develop standards tailored to SMEs.)

State-Owned Enterprises

In contrast, the statutory framework for SOEs is generally not stringent enough, considering the importance of these entities and the services they deliver. The standards that govern SOEs are frequently not as rigorous as those covering other kinds of PIEs. The Organisation for Economic Co-operation and Development's Guidelines on Corporate Governance in State-Owned Enterprises recommend that SOEs "be subject to the same high quality accounting and auditing standards as listed companies"

Box 2.2

IFRS for SMEs

A consensus has developed among policy makers and practitioners that SMEs should be subject to a simpler set of standards than PIEs, as learning and following full IFRS is very burdensome for the typical SME (the fully bound IFRS 2008 is a 2,700-page tome). Indeed, the International Accounting Standards Board (IASB) has been working since 2005 to develop "IFRS for SMEs" (also called "IFRS for Private Entities"). These standards were released in July 2009, as this book went to press. As the IASB explains on its Web site,

> Because full IFRSs were designed to meet the needs of equity investors in companies in public capital markets, they cover a wide range of issues, contain a sizeable amount of implementation guidance and include disclosures appropriate for public companies. Users of the financial statements of private entities do not have those needs, but, rather are more focused on assessing shorter-term cash flows, liquidity and solvency. Also, many private entities say that full IFRSs impose a burden on them—a burden that has been growing as IFRSs have become more detailed and more countries have begun to use them. Thus, in developing the proposed IFRS for SMEs, IASB's twin goals were to meet user needs while balancing costs and benefits from a preparer perspective.

These reduced financial reporting standards could be a boon to Latin America; indeed, El Salvador has already adopted them prospectively. Yet it remains to be seen whether these standards will be suitable for companies at the smaller end of the spectrum. Many European observers have expressed their sense that the standards in their current draft form are more applicable for medium entities than small ones. In any case, the adoption of this new standard will require an investment in capacity building that most countries have not yet contemplated. Many SMEs are unlikely to have the human and financial resources to implement it successfully without some external assistance. Furthermore, the professional accounting bodies in emerging economies often lack the capacity to initiate the comprehensive training that will be needed to effectively implement IFRS for SMEs.

(OECD 2005, 16)—a standard that remains largely unmet in LAC. Often the requirements for a particular SOE are set out in the law that created that SOE (for example, organic law), so that different requirements may apply to different SOEs in the same country. Also, since not all SOEs are required to be set up as companies proper, general commercial laws (for example, commercial code or other company laws) may not apply to them. In general, the sector suffers from a lack of transparency and accountability, as SOEs' financial statements are often not accessible to the general public (see table 2.3).[8]

In a number of LAC countries, SOEs follow a significantly different set of accounting, audit, reporting, and internal control rules than do their private sector counterparts. These standards, usually designed with a focus on government budgetary execution, are not suited for commercial entities. In addition, SOEs are often exempted from the requirement of an external audit by an independent auditor; they tend instead to be audited by a supreme audit institution (SAI), but the quality and frequency of such audits vary considerably. SAIs are often unable to conduct yearly audits of SOEs, and, in most cases, they follow government auditing standards, which focus on monitoring compliance with the national budget, rather than the broader scope of an independent external audit (OECD 2005, 42–3). In some cases, the only SOEs that are subject to an external audit are those that receive international donor funds, because the terms of the loan or grant require the audit.

Conclusion

In general, the fundamentals of LAC country statutory frameworks are sound in terms of basic A&A requirements: in most countries, the corporate financial reporting framework contains the essential elements. However, in many countries there is regulatory fragmentation because of the many rule makers. Most countries can adapt their standards, yet the pace of the legislative and regulatory process often cannot keep up with the speed of innovations in the private sector. Finally, there are important differences in the quality of the statutory frameworks across sectors.

The quality of the statutory framework tends to be the strongest in the banking sector. In nearly all countries, banks are subject to annual statutory audits, stringent auditor requirements, and audit committee requirements that are in conformity with international good practice. The regulators charged with designing and enforcing the banking requirements tend to have strong human and financial capacity (even in countries, such as Haiti, that lack overall capacity) (Friedman and Grose 2006). The quality of the regulatory framework for listed companies is generally quite robust in those countries with well-developed securities markets. The statutory framework for listed companies in Brazil, Chile, and Panama is up to international standards; however, most countries in LAC have no significant securities market, and thus have much less sophistication in their statutory framework.

There is a trend toward reform in the region. Brazil's Novo Mercado provides an interesting example of a strategy to improve corporate financial reporting through voluntary observance of higher standards. This same strategy may not work for other countries, but it does show that creative solutions can work. In Honduras, in late 2006 the government passed a Transparency and Access to Public Information Law, which requires, among other things, that SOEs make their financial statements available to the public (Government of Honduras 2006). This important development was prompted by the fact that one of the main challenges facing the government has been controlling the high levels of public debt (much of which the government backs) and budget deficits in SOEs, particularly the public utilities. Honduras is not the only country in the region facing such a challenge, and other countries might do well to adopt a similar approach.

Notes

1. These attributes are broadly in line with the principles recommended by leading legal experts. Reed Dickerson, in his Legislative Drafting (1954, 12), states that "the most important idea in legislative drafting is to say what you mean accurately, cohesively, clearly and economically." G. C. Thornton's Legislative Drafting (1970) advocates "simplicity and precision," although he emphasizes that legislation is more art than science, and that there is no "clear cut right way and wrong way" to draft legislation. In an article about legislative drafting in the financial sector, a senior counsel in the Singapore Attorney General's office advocates an approach that is flexible, scalable, comprehensible, responsive, and enforceable (Cheu 2007).

2. The components of a complete statutory framework are based on the ROSC A&A diagnostic tool, which can be accessed at http://www.worldbank.org/ifa/rosc_aa.html. The tool is in turn based on the European Union and United States statutory frameworks, which are generally considered to be complete.

3. See, for example, the opening paragraph of Accounting Research Bulletin No. 51 (as amended by Financial Accounting Standard No. 160, issued in 2007): "There is a presumption that consolidated financial statements are more meaningful than separate financial statements and that they are usually necessary for a fair presentation when one of the entities in the consolidated group directly or indirectly has a controlling financial interest in the other entities." U.S.

Financial Accounting Standards Board, Norwalk, CT. http://www.fasb.org/pdf/fas160.pdf.

4. This applies in particular to the valuation of financial instruments (especially securities investment and credit or loan portfolios), the recognition of goodwill (valued at zero from a prudential standpoint), the recognition of general reserves (prohibited by IFRS and US Generally Accepted Accounting Principles, but probably necessary from a prudential perspective), and so forth. At the same time, whenever differences can be avoided, they should be.

5. For instance, the initiation document of the European Union's Solvency II insurance oversight project states, "Where possible, [insurance-sector prudential rules should] be based on common accounting policies to produce expenditure savings and avoid the duplication (and even multiplication) of financial reporting systems" (European Commission 1999).

6. This issue has been a problem in other parts of the world in the past. A 2003 report on convergence to or adoption of IFRS, prepared by the 6 largest international networks of audit firms, states that respondents from more than 25 countries cited the tax-driven nature of the national accounting regime as an obstacle to convergence with IFRS (Street 2003). Although this information is now out of date, it shows the pervasive nature of the problem.

7. For a timeline of IFRS revisions and other IASB projects, see Deloitte's IAS+ Web site at http://www.iasplus.com/agenda/agenda.htm.

8. This broad, general assessment, of course, does not overlook certain examples of good practice in corporate governance and transparency among SOEs (examples include the Panama Canal Authority and Interconexión Eléctrica, S.A. in Colombia).

CHAPTER 3

Preserving the Good Name of the Accounting Profession

Ensuring the Profession Can Meet

Current Challenges

The accounting and auditing (A&A) profession is built upon the collective reputation of its practitioners. Accountants and auditors provide a wide array of services—from financial statement audits to environmental sustainability reporting to certifying the results of Academy Award ("Oscar") voting. What ties these diverse services together is the role of the accountant and auditor as the guardian of the public's interest and trust. Consideration of the public's interest before the client's and the firm's interests is a defining mark of the A&A profession.[1] For instance, financial statement auditors provide assurance to shareholders and other third-party stakeholders that a company's financial statements are a proper reflection of its financial position. For this assurance to have value, the auditor must be sufficiently capable and independent from the clients to confer an unbiased judgment on their financial statements. If an auditor loses the public's confidence and trust in this ability, then the auditor's assurance no longer has value.[2] The quality of the profession's membership is therefore critical.

This chapter provides an overview of the state of the A&A profession in Latin America and the Caribbean (LAC). It describes the contours and defining features of the A&A profession in general, and discusses professional organizations at the national and international levels, and their roles in regulating the profession and enhancing its quality. Finally, drawing on the experience of the Reports on the Observance of Standards and Codes, Accounting and Auditing (ROSC A&A) program and international trends in the field, this chapter discusses the challenges the profession faces in preserving the lasting market value of its professional reputation, and the innovative solutions it has used to tackle these problems.

Structure of the A&A Profession

The A&A profession encompasses a broad range of professionals. This diversity can be described along two axes, representing the size of the firms and the sophistication of their services (figure 3.1). The size of A&A firms or practitioners varies considerably: from "Big 4" international networks,[3] to second-tier international networks and other mid-size firms with some form of international affiliation, to small and medium practices (SMPs) including specialized boutique firms, and sole practitioners. Along the other axis runs a broad range of services, ranging in sophistication from bookkeeping to audit. (This presentation of the different types of engagement and providers of A&A services is a simplification; it does not mean,

Figure 3.1 Types of Accounting and Auditing Services and Size of Firms

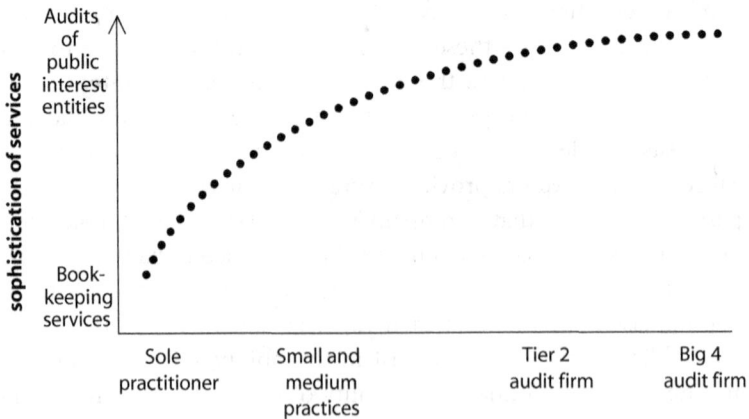

Source: Authors.

for instance, that audits could not be carried out effectively by small firms.) Although occasionally it is useful to distinguish between accountants and auditors (as this chapter does), the distinction is somewhat artificial in practice, since auditors perform accounting tasks as part of their business and (to a lesser extent) vice versa.

Role of A&A Professional Bodies

In every country, accountants and auditors have formed professional bodies to ensure minimum standards of competence and quality among their members, promote good practice among themselves, promote the role and contribution of the profession, and secure the lasting value of their professional reputation. Among the typical functions of accounting professional bodies are the following:

- Establishing education and training requirements for professional accountants and certifying that the body's membership meets these minimum requirements
- Setting standards for professional conduct and ethics as well as for auditing and other types of engagements involving some form of professional assistance (for example, reviews)
- Exercising quality control over the profession
- Sanctioning members who violate A&A standards, ethical rules, or bylaws
- Offering continuing professional development training, seminars, conferences, and publications
- Representing and promoting the interests of the profession to government institutions and other bodies.[4]

In some countries, the A&A professional body has taken on more than these activities; for example, several accounting professional bodies also serve as the official A&A standard setters.

This section discusses the challenges the national professions face and describes how they have responded to those challenges.

Lack of Revenues

One of the primary factors limiting the ability of professional bodies to improve their effectiveness is lack of financial resources. Many organizations charge their members very low dues, and have difficulty collecting even these amounts from their members; then, of course, they are unable to provide the services that entice members to pay their dues. For example, the Dominican Republic's Institute of Authorized Public Accountants (Instituto de Contadores Públicos Autorizados de la República Dominicana, or ICPARD) charges US$34 a year in membership dues, and membership in ICPARD is a legal requirement to practice as an accountant or auditor in the Dominican Republic; yet it faces severe difficulties in collecting members' dues.[5] As table 3.1 shows, professional associations around the world charge a wide range of membership dues.

Table 3.1 Membership Dues of Selected Professional Accountancy Bodies

Country	Professional body	2009 membership dues for individuals (US$)	Mandatory affiliation requirement	Approximate number of members
Brazil (State of São Paulo)	CRCSP	125	Yes	112,000
Dominican Republic	ICPARD	34	Yes	14,000
Mexico (Federal District)	CCPM	530	Yes	6,000
Paraguay	CCP	42	No	1,500
Uruguay	CCEAU	65	No	5,000
United Kingdom	ICAEW	408	No	130,000
United Kingdom	ACCA	255	No	122,000
United Kingdom	CIMA	309	No	65,000
Spain	ICJCE	750[a]	No	5,500
United States	AICPA	395	No	330,000
Canada	CGA Canada	670	No	45,000

Source: LAC ROSC A&A review and additional surveys.

Note:
a. This amount is charged to sole-practitioner members; individuals who practice as a member of a firm are charged the equivalent of $355 per year.

CRCSP	Conselho Regional de Contabilidade do Estado de São Paulo	Regional Accounting Council of the State of São Paulo
ICPARD	Instituto de Contadores Públicos Autorizados de la República Dominicana	Institute of Authorized Public Accountants of the Dominican Republic
CCPM	Colegio de Contadores Públicos de México	College of Public Accountants of Mexico
CCP	Colegio de Contadores del Paraguay	College of Accountants of Paraguay
CCEAU	Colegio de Contadores, Economistas y Administradores del Uruguay	College of Accountants, Economists, and Administrators of Uruguay
ICAEW	Institute of Chartered Accountants in England and Wales	
ACCA	Association of Chartered Certified Accountants	
CIMA	Chartered Institute of Management Accountants	
ICJCE	Instituto de Censores Jurados de Cuentas de España	Institute of Sworn Auditors of Spain
AICPA	American Institute of Certified Public Accountants	
CGA	Certified General Accountants Association of Canada	

Charging adequate dues has been a challenge in many countries. Because the cost of carrying out some typical activities (for example, maintaining a library and a Web site for the membership and the public) represents a significant fixed expenditure, the professional bodies with a larger membership enjoy a significant advantage over those with smaller ones. For instance, with a membership estimated at up to 400,000, Brazil's Federal Accounting Council (Conselho Federal de Contabilidade, or CFC) could afford to charge relatively low annual dues and still derive a rather comfortable level of revenue. By contrast, professional bodies in Paraguay, Uruguay, and the smaller Caribbean or Central American countries can only do so much with an inherently limited constituency. In some small countries (for example, the Eastern Caribbean island states), the sustainability of a professional body is an issue because of the lack of a critical mass of practitioners to absorb the necessary fixed costs of running a strong professional body (rental of office space, administrative and technical staff, and so forth).

A strong organization that provides its members with the services they want will most likely have less trouble collecting its dues (Seibert 2008). A case in point is Uruguay's College of Accountants, Economists and Administrators (Colegio de Contadores, Economistas y Administradores del Uruguay, or CCEAU), which is able to fund a wide variety of activities and an intensive program of seminars and training courses with its $65 annual membership fee. The CCEAU is better able to collect membership dues because, as the ROSC states, it "has garnered a good reputation in Uruguay and also in the rest of Latin America for its dedication to the advancement of the accounting profession." Strong accountancy professional bodies attract members and can levy significant dues because they (a) provide services that their members want and (b) increase the value of their membership by restricting it to only the most qualified practitioners.

Existence of Several Professional Associations

Another, somewhat related, source of difficulties for the profession in many countries is its lack of cohesion: it is fairly common for internal divisions within the profession to lead to factions and competing professional bodies. Approximately two-thirds of the ROSC A&A reports describe multiple professional bodies competing for members within the same countries.[6] An extreme case is Panama, which, with a population of less than 4 million, has four officially sanctioned professional bodies. Although these associations attempt to cooperate through a joint technical board, their divisions lead to inertia, conflict, and ineffective advocacy to government and other external stakeholders. Moreover, they compete for and divide among themselves a limited pool of dues-paying members, which weakens their institutional capacity. Many other countries with two or more competing professional bodies suffer from similar problems.

The multifaceted structure of the A&A profession contributes to these divisions. The market for audit services, and particularly for services to public interest entities (PIEs), is generally dominated by the local affiliates or member firms of the Big 4 global audit networks or, in a few countries (for example, Brazil and the Dominican Republic), second-tier or mid-sized firms. The professional bodies, however, tend to be dominated by representatives of smaller practices or academia. Although large audit firm partners, with their fairly integrated international network, are arguably in the best position to promote international good practice, their presence is not always welcome; thus, they lack incentives to cooperate with, and are frequently disengaged from, the national professional bodies. Even in countries where international audit firms are actively engaged in the professional bodies, their presence can be the cause of divisions within the profession, as other members (especially small practitioners) can perceive their presence as a threat. For example, until 2007, the accounting body of the city of Buenos Aires was not a member of the Argentine Federation of Professional Councils in Economic Sciences (Federación Argentina de Consejos Profesionales de Ciencias Económicas, or FACPCE). This meant that FACPCE could not access the pool of technical resources represented by the capital city's profession; it also led to the development of two competing sets of accounting standards. In mid-2007, an agreement was reached under which the Buenos Aires accounting body joined FACPCE again. Shortly thereafter, Argentina announced a series of measures to align the country's practice with international standards, including a decision to adopt International Financial Reporting Standards (IFRS) for listed companies.

Different poles within the A&A profession can complement each other. A case in point is Brazil's two professional bodies, CFC and IBRACON (IBRACON represents the large and mid-size audit firms). These two bodies generally work well together: they jointly develop Brazilian Generally Accepted Accounting Principles and Generally Accepted Auditing Standards (GAAP and GAAS), and together they have built strong ties with the business community, regulators, government, and so on. Governments cannot do much about self-inflicted wounds and divisions within the profession, but where they can encourage unity, they should.

Reserved Functions and Mandatory Affiliation Rules

In several LAC countries, A&A professional bodies have been granted certain reserved functions—for example, accountants may be the only professionals entitled to perform certain activities, such as preparing tax returns. In addition, several countries have mandatory affiliation provisions: accountants must join a professional body to practice (table 3.2).

Rules that Fall Short of International Standards of Good Practice

Although accountants and auditors share the same profession, the professional requirements to carry out their related but distinct tasks are quite different. Most LAC countries surveyed fall short of what would be considered international good practice in terms of ensuring that their auditors and accountants are sufficiently qualified. Policy makers, standard setters, and professional associations would do well to differentiate between auditing (along with other high-added-value services) and bookkeeping (or other low-added-value services) in terms of the requirements to practice and maintain a license. With a few exceptions, the A&A profession in LAC has only one tier (*contador público*), which copies the U.S. system; but its lack of differentiation has a negative, leveling effect on the

Table 3.2 Countries where Affiliation with Accounting Professional Bodies Is Mandatory

Argentina	√
Brazil	√
Chile	
Colombia	
Dominican Republic	√
Ecuador	
El Salvador	*
Haiti	√
Honduras	√
Jamaica	
Mexico	√
OECS	√
Panama	
Paraguay	
Peru	√
Uruguay	

Source: LAC ROSC A&A review.

Note: OECS = Organisation of Eastern Caribbean States.

* Registration with oversight body is required.

overall quality of the practice. Users of financial information need highly qualified auditors to attest to the reliability of the financial information. When the requirements to enter the audit profession are lower, so is the level of confidence in audited financial information.

The International Federation of Accountants (IFAC) establishes standards of good practice for its member bodies in Statements of Membership Obligations (SMOs), issued in 2004 (box 3.1). SMOs require members to make their "best endeavors" to promote, incorporate, and assist in implementing international standards issued by IFAC and the International Accounting Standards Board.[7] The SMOs also establish requirements for quality assurance and investigation and discipline activities. IFAC member bodies are theoretically bound to implement (or at least push for) adoption of IFAC's recommended standards of ethics, education, and high-quality practice.[8] Of course, bodies that are not IFAC members would also do well to adopt these standards of good practice.

The SMOs provide a clear roadmap for an accounting professional body that wants to follow good international practices. Essentially, they recom-

---

Box 3.1

IFAC Statements of Membership Obligations (SMOs)

SMO 1
Quality Assurance

SMO 2
International Education Standards for Professional Accountants and other International Auditing Education Standards Board (IAESB) guidance

SMO 3
International standards, related practice statements and other papers issued by the International Auditing and Assurance Standards Board (IAASB)

SMO 4
IFAC Code of Ethics for Professional Accountants

SMO 5
International Public Sector Accounting Standards and other International Public Sector Accounting Standards Board (IPSASB) guidance

SMO 6
Investigation and Discipline

SMO 7
International Financial Reporting Standards (IFRS)

mend the rules that their member bodies should put in place for their own members. Unfortunately, most professional bodies have not adopted these international good-practice standards: no IFAC member body in Latin America complies with all seven SMOs, and few comply with more than three. Instead of using IFAC's good-practice rules, professional associations typically have in place more limited, outdated codes of practice and ethics. To advance the regional profession, IFAC's member bodies in the region will need a serious commitment to complying with IFAC's SMOs, and IFAC itself will need strong commitment to its enforcement role.

Lack of Enforcement

The global accounting profession's tradition of self-regulation has been called into question since the beginning of this decade. In most upper-income countries, the government now plays an active role in regulating the profession, mainly in relation to the function of statutory auditor (Devlin 2006). However, this trend has not yet had a significant impact in LAC, where the accounting profession is still largely self-regulated (Thomadakis 2005).

Self-regulation means that the profession establishes its own rules and creates its own institutions and mechanisms for enforcing compliance with these rules. For example, many A&A professional bodies have established an "honor council" to receive, investigate, and punish complaints against member accountants. These honor councils are not usually proactive in reviewing adherence to ethical and quality standards, but rather respond only to specific complaints of malfeasance. Another less common arrangement is to establish a system of peer reviews to determine that accountants and (particularly) auditors are complying with professional standards. In the United States, the American Institute of Certified Public Accountants (AICPA) has had such a quality assurance peer review system in place for a long time (although its relative importance has declined since the establishment of the Public Company Accounting Oversight Board).

In only three countries reviewed (Brazil, Jamaica, and Peru) do professional bodies have active disciplinary functions; in the other countries, the professional bodies very rarely sanction their members for violations of ethical rules or failure to comply with A&A standards. Self-regulatory arrangements are problematic for several reasons. First, the leadership of most professional bodies is elected, and an elected leadership is loath to put in place a system that would in practice punish some of their members for noncompliance with required standards and rules. Second, human nature is such that even professionals charged with reviewing their peers' work and conduct may find it easier to let professional or ethical lapses slide, perhaps in hopes that they will be given the same indulgence if their performance is ever reviewed (the expression "go along to get along" captures this sentiment). In short, a system of professional self-regulation is inherently weaker than independent oversight, because there are few incentives for those charged with enforcement to insist upon compliance. This, in turn, diminishes incentives for accountants and auditors to comply with the rules (Grumet 2005).

Entry Requirements: Limits of a System Based on University Accreditation

A fundamental role of any A&A professional association is to determine requirements for entry to the profession—that is, to define who may properly call themselves accountants and auditors (IFAC 2009a). Being affiliated with a well-regarded organization with more demanding entry requirements (for example, Britain's Association of Chartered Certified Accountants, AICPA in the United States, or the CPC designation within Mexico's Institute of Public Accountants) adds to an accountant's or auditor's value because businesses recognize the difficulty of obtaining and maintaining the professional certification.

IFAC, in its International Education Standards for Professional Accountants (IES), prescribes education and training standards to ensure that accountants and auditors are highly qualified; and it includes adoption of IES among its SMOs. Broadly speaking, the IES requirements for entry to the A&A profession are as follows:

- A university education with adequate accounting curriculum standards (including ethics education)
- At least three years of practical experience under an experienced mentor
- A qualifying examination (IFAC 2008).

This section discusses each of these entry requirements and their application in LAC.

Education Requirement

Most LAC countries require only a university degree in accounting to practice as an accountant or as an auditor.[9] However, a university degree in accounting does not by itself ensure that the holder is a qualified accountant, much less an auditor. One of the main problems with this requirement is that minimum curriculum standards for the accounting degree are uneven across the region, and they do not tend to keep up with global A&A trends (see chapter 4). University accounting departments should strive to fulfill the curriculum requirements set forth in the IES, which are fairly detailed in describing the areas of accounting, auditing, finance, economics, and other topics that should be covered.

Professional Experience Requirement

Auditing is a skill that must be honed over time—an auditor gains invaluable judgment with each engagement. For this reason, the IES and international best practice dictate that auditors be required to gain at least three years of relevant practical experience under the guidance of a qualified auditor before they can be certified as auditors themselves (IFAC 2008). In general, LAC countries recognize the value of relevant professional experience. Although most countries do not require such experience of all auditors, they do typically require it from auditors of supervised entities (table 3.3). A few countries, rather than mandating relevant experience, only require a certain number of years of membership in the professional body; this is not in line with the IES.

Entry Examination Requirement

The professional examination (or series of examinations) is a critical tool for evaluating candidates for certification as an auditor. It is one of the most objective ways to evaluate a candidate's knowledge and preparedness to be an accountant and an auditor. All of the internationally recognized accounting credentials use an exam to evaluate candidates, and guidelines for the content of a professional accounting exam are set forth in IFAC's IES. Unfortunately, this tool is underutilized in LAC—only the accounting professional bodies in Haiti and Mexico administer a professional accounting examination, and only the Mexican examination is considered sufficiently rigorous to meet the IES requirements.[10]

Requirements to Maintain a Professional License

Once accountants or auditors have been licensed to practice, it is important that they keep their skills up to date through continuing professional development (CPD). Innovations in business lead to changes in the A&A regime, and an effective practitioner needs to renew his or her knowledge base constantly.

Table 3.3   Professional Experience Requirements for Statutory Auditors

Country	Years	Comment
Argentina	0	Three years of experience in audit to register as an external auditor for listed companies, banks, or insurance companies. Otherwise, no professional experience required to audit.
Brazil	0	
Chile	0	Three or five years of experience required to audit a large, "registered" company (depending on type of post-secondary degree obtained).
Colombia	1	
Dominican Republic	0	
Ecuador	0	
El Salvador	0	
Haiti	0	Five years of experience or a university diploma are substitutable for the entry examination.
Honduras	0	
Jamaica	2.5	
Mexico	0	A candidate must wait for three years but is not required to gain practical work experience.
OECS	3	
Panama	0	
Paraguay	3	
Peru	0	Must be a member of a Colegio for five years (no requirement to gain practical experience).
Uruguay	0	Central Bank's auditor registry does require professional and specific sectoral experience to audit supervised entities, but no overall experience requirement to become an auditor of other entities.

Source: LAC ROSC A&A review.

Continuing Professional Development

For accountants to keep pace with evolving accounting standards driven by innovations in commerce and finance, IFAC's IES require at least 120 hours of CPD for each 3-year period (or an average of 40 hours per year). All of the internationally recognized accounting certifications require a similar number of CPD hours. However, most LAC professional associations fall short of this standard (table 3.4), although the growing number of organizations that have adopted some CPD requirement is encouraging. Several ROSCs raised questions about the enforcement of CPD requirements, which appears to be lax in most cases.

Professional Ethics: Maintaining Independence and Serving the Public Interest

Financial statement users rely on auditors and accountants to be not only competent, but also fair and unbiased. Policy makers and the profession

Table 3.4 CPD Hours Required per Year

Argentina	0
Brazil	32
Chile	0
Colombia	0
Dominican Republic	0
Ecuador	0
El Salvador	0
Honduras	0
Haiti	35[a]
Jamaica	65
Mexico	40
OECS	30
Panama	0
Paraguay	50
Peru	20
Uruguay	0

Source: LAC ROSC A&A review.

Note:
a. There is some uncertainty as to whether this requirement is valid.

therefore need to establish rules to guide accountants and auditors in meeting challenges to their independence. For example, auditors and their firms should not have a financial or other interest in the companies they are auditing; best practice generally prohibits the firm and all of its employees from owning any interest whatsoever in a client company (IFAC 2005). In addition, as the public saw in the wake of the Enron scandal and others like it, it is important that audit work be strictly separated from advisory assistance or other engagements that can present a conflict of interest.

Potential threats to auditor and accountant independence are legion, however. IFAC's comprehensive 2005 Code of Ethics classifies the various threats to accountant and auditor objectivity into five major categories, provides a framework for judging whether a particular situation or factor could threaten an accountant's or an auditor's impartiality, and recommends specific safeguards to preserve independence from these threats.

A comprehensive code of ethics with situation-specific guidance is indispensable for delineating clear guidelines and disciplining professionals who commit ethical breaches. Adopting IFAC's Code of Ethics is considered good practice and is also required under IFAC's SMOs. Yet the ROSC reviews have found that many LAC professional bodies, even some that are IFAC members, have not adopted IFAC's Code of Ethics. Instead, they frequently develop their own, more limited codes of ethics, in which the concept of serving the public interest frequently goes unmentioned. The independence requirements typically detailed in a national code of ethics in LAC tend to be limited in scope, and in most countries they go unenforced.

Auditor rotation is another important systemic tool for preserving auditor independence. In most cases, companies are required to periodically rotate the signing partner of the audit engagement (five years is a common period). This practice (adopted in the United States under the Sarbanes-Oxley Act and in the European Union under the Eighth Directive on Company Law) has been adopted in supervised sectors of most countries in the LAC region, and several countries report that they are moving toward auditor rotation. Brazil and Paraguay require companies to rotate their audit *firm*;[11] that is, companies must hire a new company to audit their financial statements, rather than simply change the signing partner. Although audit partner or firm rotation is useful, it is not sufficient in itself to ensure auditor independence.

Regulation and Oversight of the Statutory Audit Function

In the absence of strong self-regulation by the accountancy profession, PIE regulators (banking supervisors, nonbank financial sector supervisors, securities market regulators, and supreme audit institutions) have put in place requirements to promote high-quality audits in their sectors. As many regulators rely on external auditors to uncover areas of risk or irregularities in the financial statements of regulated entities (Basel Committee on Banking Supervision 2008), most LAC countries have taken some steps to ensure that statutory auditors of PIEs meet a minimum threshold of competence. At a minimum, regulators may reserve the right to approve or disapprove of the choice of external auditor, and they may require prior sectoral experience (for example, Uruguay's Central Bank requires previous experience for prospective auditors of banks, insurance companies, pension funds, or other financial institutions). Other supervisors keep registries of approved auditing firms or individuals (box 3.2 shows how two such registries work in practice). In some countries, different supervisors maintain separate registries of approved external auditors, which can be a source of confusion and needless duplication of effort. The Dominican Republic has four separate registries of approved auditors—for banks, insurance companies, pension funds, and listed companies. Since the requirements to qualify as external auditors should be similar, supervisors should seek to streamline these requirements by sharing information and centralizing their registries.

Box 3.2

Statutory Auditor Registries in Argentina and Honduras

Argentina:
Central Bank's Department of Auditor Control

External auditors play an essential role with regard to the accuracy and trustworthiness of financial reporting by financial institutions. Since 1998, consistent with an approach endorsed by the Basel Committee on Banking Supervision, Argentina's Central Bank has taken several steps to ensure that external auditors of financial institutions not only are properly qualified but also effectively observe high standards of audit practice. In particular, the Central Bank established the Department of Auditor Control (DAC), which is responsible for supervising external auditors and audit committees. On average, DAC conducts some 60 inspections per year of external audits of financial institutions, giving external auditors a grade of 1 to 5. Firms with the lowest grade (unacceptable) are excluded from the registry of approved external auditors. Argentina's experience illustrates a growing trend among banking supervisors to leverage the work of external auditors as part of a supervision strategy focusing on risks. It is also an interesting example of how financial sector regulators can play a meaningful role in monitoring the quality of the audit practice in their jurisdiction.

Honduras:
National Banking and Insurance Commission's Auditor Registry

The National Banking and Insurance Commission of Honduras (Comisión Nacional de Bancos y Seguros, or CNBS) uses a four-tier classification system for its auditor registry, and classifies firms into one of the four categories. A firm is authorized to audit institutions in its category or lower (that is, a Category C audit firm may audit all companies in its category as well as in Category D). The classification system is as follows:

A: Banks and insurance companies

B: Private pension funds, rating agencies, leasing companies, non-banking financial institutions

C: Insurance brokers, bonded warehouses, foreign exchange operators, stock brokerage firms, microfinance institutions

D: Large corporate borrowers

To register, audit firms must submit to CNBS information about the firm, its partners and staff, and its clients. CNBS reviews their qualifications and assigns them a category. Auditors in categories A, B, and C are required to take out professional liability insurance. The registration must be renewed annually.

Another alternative for identifying qualified external auditors for regulated entities is to work with the profession to create a more rigorous certification for auditors. Mexico has done this with the adoption of the Contador Público Certificado (CPC) accreditation: the supervisors of banks, other financial institutions, and listed companies require that external auditors of supervised entities hold the CPC accreditation.

Independent Oversight of Statutory Auditors: A Key Element of a Modern Framework

It is clear that the accountancy profession and the government share an interest in identifying and certifying highly qualified independent auditors. Recognizing independent auditors' distinctive responsibilities toward the public and the consequent need to monitor audit practice and ensure that financial statement audits meet acceptable levels of quality, countries throughout the world have begun to replace self-regulation with public oversight boards whose responsibilities include registering statutory auditors, setting audit and professional ethics standards, enforcing professional standards through inspections, and reporting to the public.

Examples of independent auditor oversight boards abound: Canada's Public Accountability Board, France's Haut Conseil du Commissariat aux Comptes, Spain's Instituto de Contabilidad y Auditores de Cuentas, the UK's Financial Reporting Council (FRC), and the U.S. Public Company Accounting Oversight Board (PCAOB). In the developing world, countries such as Mauritius and Sri Lanka have established entities with similar functions.[12] Indeed, the International Forum of Independent Audit Regulators (IFIAR), founded in 2006, now has more than 30 member organizations.[13] Brazil's securities market regulator (Comissão de Valores Mobiliários) is the only Latin American member institution at this writing, although it is not technically an audit oversight board.

Good practice dictates that a majority of the independent audit oversight board's members should be nonpractitioners; rather, they should be representatives of regulatory agencies and other concerned public institutions (for example, academia, the financial community, and civil society groups).[14] Nominations should follow a process provided in the law or the board's bylaws.

Although the concept of independent audit oversight boards is beginning to take hold in LAC, the model is a challenging one to implement. Among the most significant challenges is ensuring that the board is adequately funded: who should bear the burden of the costs of these institutions? The PCAOB's revenues are provided mostly from securities-issuing companies, based on their market capitalization, and from the registration and annual fees it charges public accounting firms.[15] In the United Kingdom, a debate is now underway over FRC's proposal to levy increased charges on listed companies, pensions, and insurance firms to pay for its oversight. The national government covered one-third of the costs until 2008, when it withdrew, leaving market participants to cover most costs.[16] (Box 3.3 describes El Salvador's experience with an independent oversight board.)

Box 3.3

El Salvador's Independent Audit Oversight Board

El Salvador's Accounting and Auditing Professional Oversight Board (Consejo de Vigilancia de la Profesión de Contaduría Pública y de Auditoría, or CVPCPA) is the region's primary example of an independent audit oversight board.[a] It is a six-member board: the President is appointed by the Ministry of Economy, one member by the Ministry of Finance, one by the National Association of Private Enterprise, one by the financial system supervisor and the stock market regulator, jointly, and one by each of the two accounting professional associations.

CVPCPA's experience highlights a key challenge in implementing an independent audit oversight board: putting in place sufficient human and financial resources for effective operation. CVPCPA has a technical staff of four and an administrative staff of five, with select members of the profession contributing their time on a pro bono basis. It does not have a permanent executive, and its annual budget of US$110,000 (for 2004) is provided entirely by the state. Furthermore, most members are practicing accountants, which raises independence concerns. Elements of this institution are admirable—its multidisciplinary nature and its authority to set and enforce A&A standards—but it needs considerable strengthening to be effective. El Salvador, and other countries in the region that follow the CVPCPA's lead, will need to identify innovative solutions to the lack of resources and other challenges.

a. CVPCPA's role includes (a) registering public accountants (including auditors); (b) overseeing the professional practice; (c) setting minimum requirements for auditing, and monitoring compliance by auditors; (d) setting accounting and financial reporting standards and authorizing internationally accepted accounting principles and auditing standards; (e) issuing a professional ethics code; (f) investigating any complaint regarding noncompliance with legal requirements and professional practice; and (g) promoting continuing education among public accountants.

Placing the burden on listed companies does not seem politically feasible in most LAC countries, which do not have large stock exchanges with enough companies to support such institutions. Given the public's interest in sound and transparent financial reporting, and the public-good nature of reliable corporate financial information, national governments will likely continue to play a role in establishing and fostering independent audit oversight boards, especially in emerging-market countries.

A strong case could therefore be made that the government and the profession should share most of the costs, since independent audit oversight boards help to improve the overall quality and reputation of the profession. However, the largest firms maintain that they have their own internal quality-control procedures, and they do not appear willing to fund a quasigovernmental institution to oversee the profession as a whole. In any case, no oversight board is currently funded solely through contributions by the profession.

Independent oversight boards are being established around the world. Countries in LAC seeking applicable models could look to the Mauritius Financial Reporting Council, the Sri Lanka Accounting and Auditing Standards Monitoring Board, or the South African Independent Regulatory Board for Auditors. It is to be hoped that IFIAR will soon begin to see more membership applications from independent audit oversight boards in LAC.

Role of International Organizations and Regional Cooperation

National institutions are not the only actors with a role in strengthening the A&A profession in LAC. Regional and international A&A organizations already enjoy a significant presence in the region, and there is room for them to exercise further leadership in the development of the profession.

IFAC will continue to play a prominent role in providing leadership for the profession's development at the country and regional levels. Through its standard-setting activities in the areas of auditing, education, ethics, and public sector financial reporting, IFAC provides best-practice guidance to accountancy professional bodies around the world. IFAC's Member Body Compliance program, based on self-assessments, serves as a basis for suspending or expelling members. The program has suspended IFAC members in LAC for lack of participation in the program, and one member has resigned rather than participate in the compliance program.[17] Stronger enforcement of SMOs is another way that IFAC could effect positive change in the region.

IFIAR provides interested LAC countries with the opportunity to learn international best practices from independent audit oversight boards from around the globe. As more countries establish these boards, IFIAR's leadership will be critical in recommending solutions to some of the challenges associated with implementation.

The regional accounting association, the Inter-American Accounting Association (Asociación Interamericana de Contabilidad, or AIC), was founded in 1949 as a regularly occurring regional conference and in 1971 as a permanent institution. It produces a monthly newsletter containing articles of a very general nature, organizes a conference every two years, and has cosponsored (with the Spanish management accounting professional body) a now out-of-print publication on management accounting in Latin America.

While AIC is an important forum for dialogue within the region's profession, it suffers from several weaknesses. First, its governance structure does not promote broader accountability to the public interest; rather, it is responsible only to its board of directors and, in turn, to its member professional organizations. An organization that depends for funding and leadership primarily on other underfunded and institutionally weak organizations cannot thrive. Meanwhile, AICPA and the Canadian Institute of Chartered Accountants have left the organization's membership, compounding the problem. AIC's organizational structure stands in contrast to IFAC's structure, in which a multilateral Public Interest Oversight Board (PIOB) oversees IFAC's standard-setting and compliance activities to ensure that these activities are "properly responsive to the public interest."[18] A related problem for AIC is its chronic revenue shortage: its dues collections are too low to support its range of activities. Similar organizations in other regions, such as the Confederation of Asian and Pacific Accountants and the Eastern Central and Southern African Federation of Accountants, face analogous challenges. By contrast, Europe's regional association, the European Federation of Accountants (Fédération des Experts Comptables Européens, or FEE) plays a meaningful role in coordinating the actions of the different national associations and is widely considered to be a credible player in Europe's efforts to improve its corporate financial reporting regime. AIC will require strong leadership to put itself again on course to support the profession's development in LAC.

A strong regional body in LAC would be particularly helpful for the region's smaller professional bodies, which could benefit most from international cooperation and the resulting economies of scale. There is considerable scope for regional or subregional cooperation among professional bodies, which could work together in such areas as preparing translations of key international standards, drafting laws and regulations, and offering region-wide training. Europe's strong FEE has a voice that tends to be heard; the AIC could play a similarly productive role if it were stronger. This will depend largely on the national accounting bodies' commitment to cooperation and reform in conjunction with their respective national governments.

Conclusion

The A&A profession in LAC faces many serious challenges. In many countries the profession is fractured and disorganized; most professional bodies are underfunded, and many are ill equipped to lead their members toward adoption of new and demanding international standards. Some, however, have overcome these challenges and successfully elevated their professional requirements and can serve as models for others. Professional bodies and policy makers can learn from the experiences of their counterparts in Argentina, Brazil, Mexico, and Uruguay, and from El Salvador's experience with its independent audit oversight board.

Furthermore, international and regional stakeholders are increasingly working together to better ensure quality in the region's A&A profession. For example, the annual CReCER regional conference (CReCER is a Spanish acronym that stands for Accounting and Accountability for Regional Economic Growth) brings together stakeholders in improved corporate and public sector financial reporting from across the region and the world. Several projects on public and private sector financial reporting are being implemented through the multilateral Caribbean Regional Technical Assistance Center. And there are plans in the works for a regional Center of Excellence, based in Panama, to coordinate and lead many efforts across the region, particularly in Central America.

Notes

1. IFAC Code of Ethics for Professional Accountants, Para. 100.1: "A distinguishing mark of the accountancy profession is its acceptance of the responsibility to act in the public interest. Therefore, a professional accountant's

responsibility is not exclusively to satisfy the needs of an individual client or employer." AICPA's Code of Professional Conduct begins with similar language (ET Section 53.01).

2. The highest profile example of this principle is the former Big 5 auditing firm, Arthur Andersen, which could no longer provide auditing services in the United States and, by extension, internationally because of the reputational damage it suffered, largely as a result of the collapse of its largest client, Enron.

3. The Big 4 international audit networks are Deloitte, Ernst & Young, KPMG, and PricewaterhouseCoopers.

4. For more information on accounting professional bodies, see "IFAC Criteria and Process for Membership," (IFAC 2009b), available at http://www.ifac.org/About/Membership.php.

5. ICPARD is the main professional accounting organization in the country. Affiliation with ICPARD is mandatory, although in fact many practitioners are not affiliated.

6. Although these organizations compete for members, accountants sometimes choose to join more than one professional body.

7. IFAC states that a member body is considered to have used "best endeavors" if it could not reasonably do more than it has done and is doing to meet the particular membership obligation.

8. In 2005, shortly after issuing the SMOs, IFAC initiated a program to monitor its membership's compliance with the SMOs. The Compliance Program entails, first, a self-assessment of progress in meeting Membership Obligations and, second, developing an action plan to address areas of weakness determined through the self-assessment. IFAC states that its members are not deemed noncompliant with the SMOs "as long as there is an agreed action plan and timetable for achieving compliance and progress against the plan can be demonstrated."

9. Jamaica and the Organization of Eastern Caribbean States require their auditors to possess an accounting credential from an internationally recognized organization, such as ACCA (UK), AICPA (US), or CGA (Canada). ACCA does not require a university degree, however. Students who complete the UK-based Certificate of Accounting Technician program may enter the ACCA program. Nonetheless, the ACCA credential is considered perhaps the most difficult to obtain and maintain. Haiti requires its auditors to pass a certification examination, but they may be exempted from this requirement if they possess a university degree or have at least five years of professional practice.

10. Brazil had instituted an examination (CFC's "Sufficiency Exam") in 2000; however, it has been suspended since 2005 by a court decision.

11. Brazil's Central Bank has suspended its audit firm rotation requirement, but listed companies are still subject to audit firm rotation.

12. See Mauritius Financial Reporting Council (http://www.frc.mu) and the Sri Lanka Accounting and Auditing Standards Monitoring Board (http://www.slaasmb.org).

13. For more information on IFIAR and its member organizations, see http://www.ifiar.org.

14. Sarbanes-Oxley Act of 2002, Title 1, Section 101(e) prohibits any of the PCAOB members from receiving payments or sharing in the profits from any public accounting firm, and from engaging in any other professional or business activity. Moreover, the Chair of the PCAOB may not have been a practicing accountant within the last five years prior to his or her appointment to the Board.

15. Sarbanes-Oxley Act of 2002, Title 1, Section 102(f) and Section 109.

16. For more about the debate on specific funding arrangements for the FRC, see http://www.frc.org.uk/about/funding.cfm.

17. See http://www.ifac.org/ComplianceProgram: "The program's primary objective is one of encouragement and improvement."

18. The PIOB oversees IFAC's so-called Public Interest Activity Boards: the International Auditing and Assurance Standards Board, International Accounting Education Standards Board, International Ethics Standards Board for Accountants, their respective Consultative Advisory Groups, and the Compliance Advisory Panel (CAP). The PIOB (a) reviews and approves terms of reference for these entities; (b) evaluates the boards' due process procedures; (c) oversees the work of IFAC's Nominating Committee and approves the committee's nominations to the standard-setting boards and the CAP; and (d) suggests projects to be added to the boards' work programs. The Chair of the PIOB also has the right to attend and to speak at IFAC Board meetings (http://www.ipiob.org).

CHAPTER 4

The Role of Education Systems

Preparing the Next Generation to Deliver
High-Quality Accounting

In any country, a strong education system is the foundation for a well-trained accounting and auditing (A&A) profession. High-quality accounting education underpins every other topic covered in this book—for instance, well-trained accountants are able to adhere to international A&A standards, or to serve as effective regulators of the financial or other sectors. They inspire confidence in the lenders, investors, and others who rely on the financial information that they help generate. It would not be responsible to discuss policy changes or reforms in the A&A sector without involving members of academia in the dialogue. Educators are responsible for ensuring that the next generation of accountants and auditors is prepared for the challenges of the modern business environment, so it behooves policy makers to ensure that the educators themselves are well equipped to teach effectively.

Future accountants need a solid grounding in the fundamentals of financial reporting and a familiarity with a broad range of other topics if they are to keep up with the innovations and developments that will inevitably affect corporate financial reporting during their careers. It is no longer enough to learn the basics of bookkeeping and tax principles. A modern accounting curriculum requires training in, among other subjects, management information systems, principles of corporate governance and their application, international business trends, and business ethics (IFAC 2008). Moreover, as in other professions, such as law and medicine, the pace of change in the business environment and financial innovation requires accountants to be lifelong learners. A critical component of any accounting education system, therefore, is the availability and quality of continuing professional development (CPD) training courses.

This section focuses on higher education in accounting—that is, tertiary degree programs, both specific accounting degrees and more general degrees (such as business, with an accounting specialization) that may be offered at universities or nonuniversity institutions.[1] (CPD programs and other forms of nonacademic education are covered in chapter 3.) It draws on several sources of information, particularly the 17 Reports on the Observance of Standards and Codes, Accounting and Auditing (ROSC A&A) conducted in Latin America and the Caribbean (LAC), and a review of accounting education issues in Latin America. As part of this review, questionnaires about accounting curricula, faculty, and students were sent to approximately 70 universities with accounting programs in 15 countries; 30 universities from 14 countries responded. Of these, 57 percent had a full-time accounting program at the undergraduate level, and one-third had a part-time program. The responses shed light on several challenges LAC universities are facing, and they support the findings of the ROSC A&As that were conducted thus far and much of the available literature. However, since the sample was relatively small and certain countries were overrepresented, one should be careful about generalizing the findings to all accounting programs in the region.

Recent Trends in Higher Education

Burgeoning demand for higher education in LAC has resulted in the rapid growth and expansion of private universities and other institutions: tertiary enrollment more than doubled between 1985 and 2002. LAC countries have approached the expansion of higher education in different ways. In some countries (for example, Argentina, Mexico, Uruguay, and República Bolivariana de Venezuela), public universities have expanded and diversified their enrollment. However, since governments are unable to meet the growing demand on their own, private institutions have become major providers of tertiary education; in fact, private investment in education is rising more rapidly than public funding. This has resulted in the diversification, privatization, and commercialization of higher education and its funding sources. On average, more than 40 percent of tertiary enrollment in LAC is now in private institutions; and in Brazil, 88 percent of higher education institutions were private in 2002 (Holm-Nielsen et al. 2005).

For the most part, recent trends in accounting education in Latin America mirror those in higher education more generally. In the countries assessed under the ROSC A&A, most accounting programs were offered by private institutions; and approximately two-thirds of the universities that responded to the survey are private. (Figure 4.1 shows how the private supply of higher education has evolved from 1985 to 2002.)

Figure 4.1 Private Enrollment in Latin America and the Caribbean as a Percentage of Total Enrollment (1985–2002)

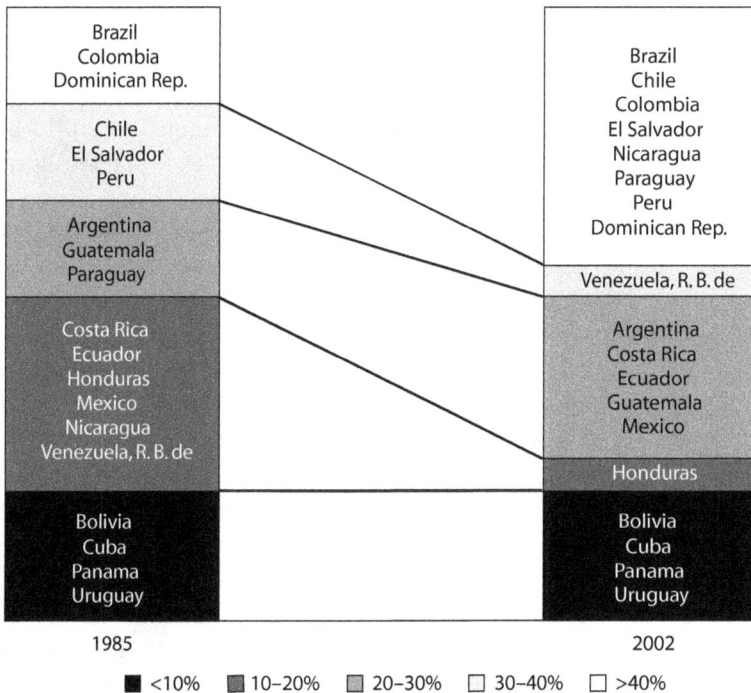

Source: Holm-Nielsen et al. 2005 (adapted).

In some countries, rapid growth from a few large universities to a large number of them has significantly changed the landscape of higher education. For example, in Panama there were only two universities—the University of Panama and the Catholic University of Santa María la Antigua—until 1980; but since 1981, more than 35 universities have been accredited to offer courses. Likewise, only two accounting degrees were offered in Panama until the 1980s, and now there are approximately a dozen. Naturally, the quality of these programs varies considerably (Borgonovo 2009).

The trend toward private provision of higher education has been generally positive, resulting in significantly expanded access to and diversification of tertiary education programs. However, there have also been negative consequences, such as greater heterogeneity across education providers (which include universities and nonuniversity institutions) and higher levels of fragmentation in education systems. Consequently, the quality of education has become increasingly uneven (Holm-Nielsen et al. 2005).

Monitoring Quality in Higher Education Systems

The challenge for governments is to ensure quality and consistency in the education provided to students. Measures have included certification and accreditation processes for tertiary degree programs (ex ante measures) and evaluations (ex post measures, for example, examinations). Ideally, governments use a combination of both ex ante and ex post controls. The use of accreditation processes has been growing in the region; several countries (for example, Argentina, Brazil, Chile, Colombia, and Uruguay) have been using them to limit the proliferation of new tertiary education institutions (Fernández Lamarra 2006). In Argentina, the National Commission for University Evaluation and Accreditation is responsible for accrediting university programs considered to be of public interest by the Ministry of Education. Accounting, recently added to the list of public interest programs, will be assessed for the first time in or around 2010, against standards issued by the Council of Deans for Economic Sciences. Universities that do not meet minimum requirements are required to submit an action plan for improvement or lose their accreditation. Universities must go through the accreditation process every six years.

The ex post evaluation of tertiary education institutions has also become more prevalent in the region (Fernández Lamarra 2006). One example is Brazil's National Examination of Student Performance (Exame Nacional de Desempenho de Estudantes, or ENADE), instituted in 2004 for students completing their first and final years of undergraduate study, to gauge how much they have learned over the course of their undergraduate studies.[2] Each year, a number of undergraduate programs are selected for evaluation, and all programs are evaluated every three years. Accounting students were evaluated for the first time under the ENADE in 2006, and a second evaluation is scheduled for November 2009. The results of the examination, disaggregated by institution, are made public (individual students' scores are not). The ENADE complements ex ante accreditation processes.[3]

It is especially important to ensure good quality in accounting education programs at the tertiary level in LAC, as few countries require anything beyond a tertiary degree as a condition to obtain a professional license of public accountant or statutory auditor. The International Education Standards for Professional Accountants (IES) issued by the International Federation of Accountants (IFAC), which are broadly considered to be the benchmark of good practice in this area, provide that, in addition to a university degree, individuals should also acquire at least three years of practical experience and pass a qualifying examination to be allowed to enter the audit profession. Only a handful of LAC jurisdictions assessed under the ROSC A&A program require a professional entry examination for auditors[4] (Haiti, Mexico, and the Organization for Eastern Caribbean States), and fewer than half have a professional experience requirement. Thus, for many countries, an undergraduate degree in accounting is the only effective prerequisite for entering the profession and performing statutory audits. One impediment to applying IES in the region is that, until very recently, they had not been translated into Spanish or Portuguese; thus, they have not been disseminated in academic circles, and their application has been very limited. The World Bank has now prepared a Spanish translation, which is being released as this book goes to print.

Course Content and Quality of Accounting Curricula

Accounting curricula in LAC tend to be of uneven quality and not up to date with some of the important developments in the field of corporate financial reporting. In two-thirds of the countries analyzed as part of the ROSC A&A, university accounting curricula did not reflect such important issues as the application of International Financial Reporting Standards (IFRS) to complex transactions (for example, issues pertaining to derivatives and other financial instruments, and the related fair value accounting), professional standards of ethics and the types of ethical dilemmas accountants and auditors may face in their professional life, and the role of accountants and auditors in the corporate governance framework. In addition, since most universities are autonomous in defining the content of their degree programs, both the content of courses and the quality of the offerings vary greatly across schools. This may reflect a broader issue regarding education in LAC: curricula have traditionally been seen as mere plans of study or lists of courses, rather than as an integral part of the academic reform process; thus, historically, the content of courses in all fields of study, not just in accounting, has been given little attention in the region (Didriksson 2008).

This section draws on the findings of the questionnaire to illustrate the gap between the contents of accounting curricula at LAC universities and international good practice as reflected in the model curriculum of the Intergovernmental Working Group of Experts on International Standards of Accounting and Reporting (UNCTAD-ISAR) and IFAC's IES. It is important to note, however, that these findings are based on self-assessments, and most universities did not submit course syllabi for verification. Thus, as with any self-assessment, there is the risk of upward bias: curriculum coverage may seem to be more comprehensive than it actually is. A recent World Bank project in Central America conducted a thorough review of accounting curricula in 11 universities in 4 countries[5] and found, for example, that while several universities reported that all relevant issues relating to IFRS were well covered, a number of subjects were missing (for example, conceptual framework for the preparation and presentation of financial statements, deferred taxes, and provisioning). Furthermore, much of the bibliography was out of date—for example, references were made to textbooks on IFRS that were edited before 2004, when significant changes were made to the standards.

General Curriculum Coverage

A high-quality accounting curriculum should be fairly broad-based, not only providing core A&A skills, but also giving students a solid understanding of the importance of reliable accounting, auditing, and reporting for well-functioning business and public sectors. Thus, curricula should include coursework in business management, economics, public finance, public administration, and ethics. Since companies frequently rely on information systems to conduct their business and keep track of their operations, successful accountants must also be familiar with management information systems and other relevant uses of information technology. It is good practice for universities to require English, which has become nearly essential when working with businesses that operate internationally. UNCTAD's model curriculum for accounting education[6] (UNCTAD-ISAR 2003) and IFAC's IES (IFAC 2008) are useful guides to designing a strong accounting curriculum; indeed, the local accounting professional bodies that are members of IFAC are required by Statement of Membership Obligations 2 to pursue the implementation of IES in their country (chapter 3).

Overall, universities reported that most core accounting subjects (that is, basic accounting, management accounting, and auditing) are well covered, while other subjects such as corporate governance and economics are often not offered as part of the accounting curriculum. This suggests that while students may be getting training in the technical aspects of accounting and audit, they may not be given an adequate sense of the role of accounting in the broader context of private and financial sector growth and development, financial transparency, and public financial management. Furthermore, in most LAC countries accounting is a degree program in itself, rather than a specialization within a more general degree such as Business Administration (as in the United States); this further limits exposure to courses in related areas. A program focused only on technical aspects of accounting is adequate to prepare a student for a career in bookkeeping. However, in almost all LAC countries, there is only one program—accounting—which educates future bookkeepers, corporate accountants, and auditors, with no differentiation in curriculum. Figure 4.2 illustrates the average coverage given to various subjects; it shows that international business and corporate governance, in particular, receive limited coverage.

Curricular heterogeneity across universities is evident in the number of class hours dedicated to any particular subject (illustrated in table 4.1). Universities vary a great deal in the amount of class time dedicated to different subjects, and some subjects are missing entirely from the curriculum: corporate governance is absent from one-third of curricula, international business from one-fifth, and ethics from 12 percent.

International Standards of Accounting and Auditing

Most universities reported course offerings in international A&A standards; however, the ROSC A&A teams have found that these courses may not be comprehensive enough to give students an adequate understanding of the subject matter. Most universities seem to recognize the need to educate students about international standards: two-thirds offer a course

Figure 4.2   Coverage of Accounting Curricula in LAC

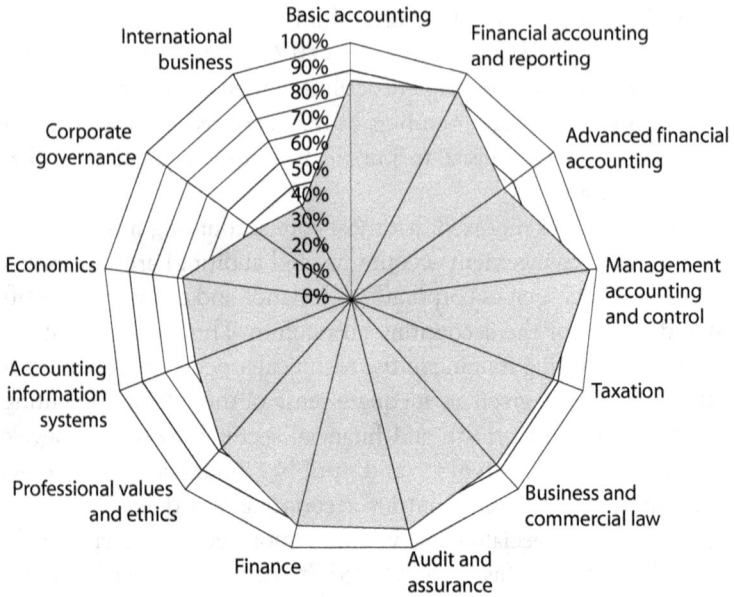

Source: Authors.

Table 4.1   Accounting Curriculum Composition in Sampled Universities

| Subject | Number of class hours per semester | | |
	Mean	Minimum	Maximum
Basic accounting	88.3	40	187
Financial accounting	106.5	43	224
Advanced financial accounting	94.7	40	192
Management accounting and control	93.4	40	200
Taxation	74.7	20	160
Business and commercial law	69.0	32	144
Audit and assurance	98.3	32	270
Finance	102.3	48	208
Professional values and ethics	47.5	0	136
Accounting information systems	61.2	0	144
Economics	92.7	0	352
Corporate governance	37.8	0	120
International business	38.0	0	80

Source: Authors.

in IFRS and International Standards on Auditing (ISA), either as separate classes or as part of a broader class. In the vast majority of cases (85 percent for IFRS, 95 percent for ISA), these are required courses. Approximately two-thirds of universities also report having translated IFRS and ISA available in their libraries, but fewer than half have copies of the translated IFAC Code of Ethics.

Classes in international standards tend to be recent: on average, they have been offered only for the past four years. Most universities indicated their intention to expand course offerings in international standards. These findings are positive insofar as they show that universities are aware of the need for courses in these subjects. Although a qualitative analysis of the courses was not part of the scope of this study, the findings of the World Bank project in Central America and interviews conducted during the ROSC process indicate that many such courses offer only a general introduction to the standards and are not comprehensive enough to give students a working knowledge of them.[7] According to the survey for this book, the most pressing constraint to offering more and better classes in international standards was the lack of qualified professors and of literature—such as textbooks—in the local language (figure 4.3).

Figure 4.3 Constraints to Offerings in International Standards

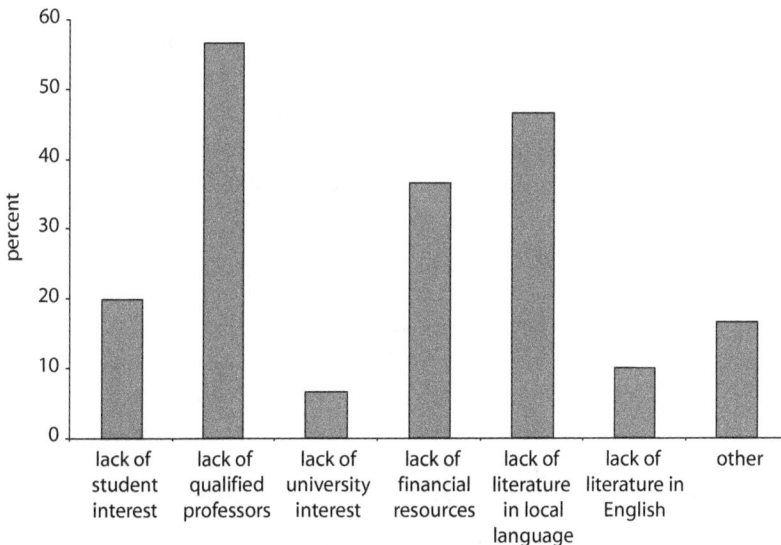

Source: Authors.

Faculty and Students

LAC students do not consider accounting programs to be very attractive. ROSC A&A interviews with academics and accounting professionals found that the accounting field tends to be viewed as less prestigious than other fields in the social sciences such as economics or business, and is therefore less attractive to higher-caliber students. Thus, in some countries (for example, Chile), the top universities do not offer an accounting program at all. The results of the survey also suggest that accounting programs tend not to be very competitive, with a median acceptance rate (the ratio of admitted students to applicants) of 76 percent.

Professors' Compensation

Of the universities surveyed, 40 percent stated that salaries are too low to attract new professors or retain current faculty. Salaries for full-time professors range from US$780 to US$3,300 per month, with a median salary of US$1,200. On average, three-quarters of faculty work only part time (the survey yielded insufficient data on salaries for part-time faculty). These low salaries have wide-ranging consequences for professors' academic effectiveness. The ROSC A&As report that professors often practice accounting to supplement their income, providing services such as bookkeeping or tax return preparation. The amount of time they devote to their practices leaves them little time for research activities. Thus, LAC universities' intellectual contribution (for example, published articles and books, comments on exposure drafts of A&A standards) is quite limited overall. And despite the apparent dissatisfaction with salaries, most universities reported having an adequate number of professors. It can therefore be inferred that the quality of the faculty may be an issue.

Professors' Qualifications

Even though close to 80 percent of universities surveyed consider their faculty to be well qualified or very well qualified, the ROSC A&A identified certain areas that need improvement. According to the survey, only about two-thirds of the professors are licensed accountants in their country—and, as chapter 3 discussed, in most LAC countries requirements for awarding a professional license are generally fairly lax (for example, no professional examination). Very few of the professors have been certified by accounting bodies that offer international certifications (for example, Canadian Chartered Accountant or Certified General Accountants Association, Mexican Contador Público Certificado, UK

Association of Chartered Certified Accountants, and U.S. Certified Public Accountant). Half of the universities reported that their professors participate in accounting conferences and seminars to refresh and update their knowledge—a positive finding, although attending those events is not sufficient to maintain up-to-date knowledge of the broad array of issues involving modern corporate financial reporting. Moreover, the quality of conferences and seminars in a number of countries is uneven.

Research and Postgraduate Education

One way for professors to keep abreast of recent developments in the field is through research, publishing, and continuing postgraduate education; however, few accounting academics in LAC are actively engaged in such activities. Only about 10 percent of universities reported that their faculty had published articles in books or journals. The survey also shows a limited offering of postgraduate programs: only one-third of surveyed universities offer a master's program in accounting, and only 20 percent offer a Ph.D. This reflects a more general problem in LAC with postgraduate programs and research activities in all fields. According to a World Bank study, postgraduate students represented only 2.4 percent of overall tertiary enrollment in LAC in 1997, compared with 12.6 percent in the United States (World Bank 2002). According to another World Bank study, "this gap can be explained partly by the low priority given to graduate and postgraduate programs, which translates into low annual Ph.D. production in Latin America" (Holm-Nielsen et al. 2005, 61). An environment that places little emphasis on research and postgraduate education presents a significant challenge for those who wish to upgrade and update professors' knowledge of modern accounting trends.

International Exposure

A&A professors, like those in any field of study, need to look beyond their immediate horizons to stay informed on their subject. Most of the key public events where issues in the accounting field are discussed are conducted in English, and they usually take place in one of the main global financial centers—New York, Washington, London, and other European capitals. But 85 percent of responding universities in LAC said that their faculty participate little or not at all in international travel or international exchange programs. Thus they have little exposure to cutting-edge issues in the field and fewer opportunities for CPD. In addition, this lack of exposure to other countries is a significant impediment to greater cooperation among academic institutions in LAC.

A lack of English language proficiency among LAC academics and students is problematic in light of the trend toward greater internationalization of the accounting field. Publications by accounting firms and professional bodies, and policy notes (such as those issued by the Public Company Accounting Oversight Board, the International Accounting Standards Board, or the European Federation of Accountants), are mostly issued only in English. Furthermore, many crucial texts for accounting academics have not been translated into Spanish (including, until recently, IFAC's IES). As a result, it is very difficult for non-English-speaking professors to keep themselves up to date on corporate financial reporting—or to participate in exchange programs with other universities in the region and in Europe or the United States, attend conferences and international academic events, and pursue international fellowships and learning sabbaticals. But among both students and faculty in the accounting discipline, proficiency in English is quite low. Most professors (55 percent) have low or very low proficiency in English; only 10 percent were considered to have a good level of proficiency; and none were considered to be excellent. Likewise, only 17 percent of undergraduate students were considered to have good or excellent English language skills, and 55 percent were considered to have low or very low proficiency.[8]

This problem suggests at least two potential responses. On the demand side, universities in Latin America may consider emphasizing English or other foreign-language ability in their accounting professors as a tool to keep abreast with continuing developments in their field. At the same time, on the supply side, international and regional organizations that produce literature and standards—IFAC; the International Accounting Standards Committee Foundation; the Inter-American Development Bank; the United Nations Conference on Trade and Development; the United Nations Educational, Scientific, and Cultural Organization; and the World Bank—need to take steps to ensure that their intended audience can access the literature. For instance, facilitating translations of international standards of accounting, auditing, and accountancy education into relevant local languages (French, Portuguese, and Spanish) would support universities' efforts to improve their curricula and the preparedness of their faculties. Most of these organizations have begun to take steps to broaden their outreach. For example, the International Accounting Standards Board (IASB) issued an exposure draft of IFRS for

SMEs (see chapter 2) in several languages,[9] and parts of IFAC's Web site have been translated into Spanish, French, Russian, Chinese, and Arabic. Still, more such efforts—particularly in partnership with the accounting academic community worldwide—would be useful.

Finally, academia has an important role to play in the international standard-setting process by providing feedback on draft standards issued by IASB and the International Auditing and Assurance Standards Board (which set IFRS and ISA, respectively). International organizations should facilitate this participation, while academics should take affirmative steps to insert themselves into the dialogue. (Since most exposure drafts are issued only in English, however, a lack of proficiency in the language remains a significant obstacle.)

Conclusion

The ROSC A&A reports and other research suggest that corporate financial reporting in LAC would benefit significantly from improved accounting education at the tertiary level. The curricula have frequently not been modernized to reflect current international standards or the model curricula developed at the international level. Underpaid professors, working just part time, often lack the time or incentives to keep abreast of these changes. In addition, limited proficiency in the English language (which, to a large extent, has become the international language of accounting) often keeps LAC students and faculties from following or engaging fully in the international dialogues that shape the profession worldwide. And international organizations could do more to include broader audiences and could disseminate their research and standards in other languages to make them more widely accessible, including in the LAC region.

Consequently, efforts to strengthen accounting education systems should come from both the supply side (efforts led by universities) and the demand side (efforts driven by the accounting profession). The following suggestions are meant to be illustrative, rather than definitive or comprehensive. Many improvements in accounting education will probably occur in the context of broader efforts to modernize tertiary education. Therefore, these suggestions are meant to contribute specifically to tertiary education in accounting.

- Supply-side efforts might involve upgrading the accounting degree curriculum to reflect internationally recognized education standards (that is, IES and UNCTAD-ISAR), or setting higher standards for faculty credentials or other qualifications, while paying higher salaries in return. Professors might be required to carry out independent research in their field, or to attend a minimum number of hours of CPD. During the hiring process, perhaps a greater emphasis could be placed on foreign-language proficiency, especially competence in English. One innovative example of a supply-side intervention to offer high-quality accounting instruction can be found in Panama's Authorized Public Accountant Specialized University (box 4.1).

- On the demand side, efforts by country authorities, the accounting profession, and the academic community to create an accounting credential on par with IES (as suggested in chapter 3), featuring a qualifying examination, would induce students to demand an accounting education that prepares them properly to pass that exam. If obtaining the credential opens doors to jobs that are unavailable to most accountants with only a bachelor's degree (such as external auditor of banks and insurance companies, or corporate controller of listed companies), then more top students will seek this higher status. Furthermore, the adoption and implementation of IFRS and other international standards would help improve the prestige of the A&A profession, and thus attract more students to the field.

- In any case, steps to improve accounting education will need to involve cooperation and assistance from a broad range of players: public institutions, accounting professional bodies, and the business community (including audit firms, financial institutions, and large companies). Countries should consider working together at a subregional level—for example, to develop a common "base" curriculum jointly or to work on common-language translations of standards. Cross-border cooperation would be particularly useful for countries that already have significant economic or trade ties (for example, countries that are signatories of the Dominican Republic–Central America Free Trade Agreement).

Box 4.1

Panama's Authorized Public Accountant Specialized University (UNESCPA)

An innovative feature of LAC's accounting education landscape is Panama's Authorized Public Accountant Specialized University (UNESCPA). It was created in 2004 by the College of Authorized Public Accountants of Panama (the *Colegio*—one of four accounting professional bodies in the country, and the only IFAC member body) and the local affiliates of the six largest international audit networks. The private institution was set up to help address a perceived lack of high-quality accounting instruction, and it is an interesting example of how international audit network affiliates can help improve the quality of the profession overall. The university offers just one four-year degree: a bachelor's degree program in accounting. It also offers master's degrees in taxation, forensic auditing, corporate finance, and banking, and certificate programs in IFRS, accounting, and finance. UNESCPA now enrolls approximately 250 students, of whom 60 are candidates for the bachelor's degree, and it plans to enroll twice as many bachelor's degree candidates in the coming years. Most of UNESCPA's professors are practitioners at the international audit firms, and the university offers instruction in IFRS, ISA, corporate social responsibility, risk-based management, forensic auditing, and information technology (including audits of information systems). Members of the *Colegio* receive discounted tuition at UNESCPA.

A comparative evaluation of UNESCPA's accounting and auditing curriculum described it as "one of the top [accounting] programs in the region," and the strongest in Panama (Borgonovo 2009). As a private, highly specialized university, UNESCPA is free from many of the obligations and challenges that confront larger and public universities. It is not yet self-sustaining, in that it relies on donations from the international audit firms. The demand for master's degree and certificate programs is reportedly strong, although the four-year program suffers from competition with other universities as well as from the greater appeal of other career paths. It is a unique example of a private sector–led, market-based initiative to address the problem of a lack of qualified accountants.

Notes

1. While the quality of primary and secondary education undoubtedly affects outcomes in accounting education, this chapter focuses on tertiary education specifically.

2. A representative sample of students is selected for mandatory participation in the examination. For more information on ENADE, see http://www.inep.gov.br/superior/enade.

3. For more on CAPES tertiary education support programs and accreditation mechanisms, see http://www.capes.gov.br.

4. Brazil had instituted an examination (CFC's "Sufficiency Exam") in 2000; however, it has been suspended since 2005 by a court decision.

5. A World Bank-managed project funded by the UK Department for International Development was carried out in 2008 to improve accounting curricula and build capacity for accounting education in five Central American countries (Costa Rica, El Salvador, Guatemala, Honduras, and Panama).

6. The model curriculum, available in English, French, and Spanish, was developed following research on technical education curricula from several countries; it is in line with IFAC's IES.

7. Of 11 universities that presented their curricula in accounting, 8 had courses in IFRS. A qualitative evaluation of the curricula of these eight universities found that the coverage of the subject matter was insufficient. In addition, as part of the ROSC A&A missions, teams interviewed a number of universities and found that many courses in international standards tended to give only a general introduction to the subject matter.

8. This issue is, of course, not limited to the accounting field. A World Bank report examining trends in Latin American education notes, "Most of the country studies identify the lack of proficiency in foreign languages among students, faculty, and staff. This has a negative impact on the international competencies of Latin American students and scholars and on their ability to take advantage of opportunities for international cooperation" (Gacel-Ávila et al. 2005, 348).

9. Specifically, Spanish, French, German, Romanian, and Polish; see http://www.iasb.org.

CHAPTER 5

Adoption of International Accounting and Auditing Standards

Seeking Harmony in a Chorus of Voices

One of the most important global trends in corporate financial reporting is the gradual move toward adopting international accounting and auditing (A&A) standards. Global investors seek the best risk-adjusted return on capital, irrespective of national borders. A uniform set of global standards not only accommodates cross-border financial flows but also positions countries and their companies to take advantage of them. Adopting internationally recognized A&A standards promotes foreign direct investment, facilitates international trade and capital flows, and helps to move toward regional integration (Hope, Jin, and Kang 2006; Covrig, Defond, and Hung 2007; Bradshaw, Bushee, and Miller 2004). Thus, countries' financial architecture is becoming increasingly globalized, including in Latin America and the Caribbean (LAC) (Diao, Díaz-Bonilla, and Robinson 2003).

Most countries in the world have adopted International Financial Reporting Standards (IFRS) for listed companies. Since 2005, all listed companies in the European Union (EU) have been required to apply IFRS for their consolidated financial statements. In addition, since 2003, IFRS and the U.S. Generally Accepted Accounting Principles (U.S. GAAP) have been on an accelerated convergence path. In November 2007, the U.S. Securities and Exchange Commission (SEC) announced that it would accept financial statements from foreign issuers prepared under full IFRS, without reconciliation to U.S. GAAP (U.S. SEC 2007). Therefore, if LAC companies listed in the United States apply IFRS, they do not need to make any additional effort to present financial statements in Europe or the United States. In November 2008, the SEC issued a proposal for comment that would require use of IFRS by U.S. securities issuers in 2014 (U.S. SEC 2008).

IFRS in LAC: Overcoming the Adopt versus Adapt Dilemma

Almost all LAC countries have adopted[1] IFRS for listed companies, in line with good international practice (table 5.1 and appendix C). Until recently, virtually every country in LAC maintained its own set of accounting standards (Casey and Masci 2003), usually crafting local standards by adapting international or U.S. accounting standards to national systems and requirements. By the middle of the present decade, although several smaller countries (the Dominican Republic, El Salvador, Honduras, Jamaica, and Uruguay) had adopted IFRS in full, the larger countries in the region continued to develop their own standards, which they felt were more amenable to their respective environments, and not as demanding as international ones. Yet even where local financial reporting standards were quite sophisticated and consistent with good practice, the differences from international standards created problems for users of international financial statements who might not be familiar with local rules (Casey and Masci 2003). By now, however, most large economies of the region (for example, Argentina, Brazil, Chile, and Mexico) have shifted their position and have officially adopted IFRS for listed companies (appendix C).[2]

Key Challenges in IFRS Adoption

LAC countries have faced a number of challenges in adopting and implementing IFRS. Adoption is only a first—relatively easy—step; the greatest difficulty comes in ensuring the effective and sustained implementation of the standards. If this is to happen, the scope of application of IFRS should be limited to companies in which there is a public interest; ample transition time should be allowed for effective implementation of the

Table 5.1   Status of IFRS Adoption by Statute in LAC Countries
(as of March 2009)

Country	Banking	Insurance	Pension funds	Listed companies[a]	SOEs	Other entities (including SMEs)
Argentina				b		
Brazil	√	√	√	√		
Chile				c		
Colombia						
Dominican Republic				√	√	√
Ecuador				d		d
El Salvador				√		e
Haiti				n.a.		
Honduras				f	√	√
Jamaica				√		
Mexico				√		
OECS				√		
Panama				√		√
Paraguay				√		
Peru				√		√
Uruguay				√	√	√

Source: LAC ROSC A&A review.

Note: n.a. = Not applicable; OECS = Organisation of Eastern Caribbean States; SOE = State-owned enterprise; SME = Small and medium enterprise.

a. Financial institutions listed on stock exchanges normally follow prudential financial reporting requirements issued by their respective supervisory agencies; these rules may differ from IFRS.

b. Except those listed on the SME segment.

c. Listed companies with a free float of 25 percent or more.

d. All entities under the supervision of the Superintendency of Companies.

e. IFRS for SMEs.

f. IFRS is required for listed, nonfinancial companies. However, at this time only financial institutions are listed on the exchange, and these follow prudential rules, issued by the Banking and Insurance Commission, that differ from IFRS.

standards; and an adequate mechanism for ensuring that "local IFRS" keep pace with new standards and amendments (issued by the International Accounting Standards Board, or IASB) is required. Finally, as the number of LAC countries that have adopted IFRS continues to grow, it becomes increasingly important for these countries to be actively engaged in the international standard-setting process, which means reviewing exposure drafts for key standards and submitting detailed comments to the IASB.

Scope of Application

In some countries, too many companies (including small and medium enterprises, or SMEs) are required to conform to international standards. The separate paths taken by smaller and larger countries in adopting IFRS created a paradoxical situation: the countries with relatively small securities markets adopted the most ambitious standards and required them for the broadest range of companies, including SMEs. As a result, these countries have struggled to equip their business communities and accounting professions to prepare financial statements according to international standards. These countries should consider relieving the burden for smaller companies, particularly for SMEs. The Reports on Observance of Standards and Codes, Accounting and Auditing (ROSC A&A) assessments in LAC recommend the adoption of full IFRS for the consolidated financial statements of public interest entities (PIEs), such as listed companies, banks, insurance companies, and pension funds. Most countries have not adopted IFRS for other types of PIEs, such as financial institutions, state-owned enterprises (SOEs) and large, nonlisted companies.

Transition Time

International experience shows that at least four years are necessary for companies, users, accountants, and regulators to prepare themselves adequately once the obligation to apply IFRS goes into effect. Successfully managing the transition to IFRS adoption requires a sustained and thorough engagement on the part of implementing authorities (such as the securities market regulator), including such activities as the following:

- Regular outreach to the business community,
- Substantial training of regulatory staff and market participants,
- Ongoing and transparent communication to ensure that the requirements and the timeframe are properly understood and can be met, and
- Close monitoring of companies' progress in preparing for implementation.

Keeping Standards Up to Date

Country authorities have often had difficulty keeping their local version of IFRS current with international standards as issued by IASB. In some countries, adoption has been viewed as a one-time event, not as a process. IFRS are a "moving target:" new standards are issued and old standards are updated continually to keep up with market conditions and demands. Financial statements prepared under out-of-date standards are not comparable with those prepared under current standards. For example, in El Salvador, the accounting standard setter decided in late 2004 to require companies to apply the 2003 version of IFRS rather than the 2004 version. Since then, IFRS have undergone two major revisions[3] as part of an improvement project launched at the request of international stakeholders.[4] Yet the law in El Salvador continues to require "IFRS 2003," which are not comparable to current IFRS; thus, it forces some users to reconcile the financial information with current standards. An additional problem is that the recently issued IFRS for SMEs (which El Salvador is poised to adopt) are based on a more recent version of the full standards.

Participating in the International Standard-Setting Process

LAC countries that have adopted or plan to adopt IFRS need to participate in the international standard-setting process, so that the standards reflect their needs and local realities. Most countries of the region do not contribute significantly to this process (table 5.2): there are very few LAC representatives on the independent boards of the IASB or the International Federation of Accountants (IFAC), which set international standards in private and public sector accounting, auditing, professional education and training, ethics, and other areas. As a result, the voice of LAC countries might not be heard when IFRS, International Standards on Auditing, International Education Standards, IFAC Code of Ethics, and International Public Sector Accounting Standards are defined. The recent appointment of a Brazilian banking supervisor to the IASB is an encouraging sign.

Table 5.2   Participation of LAC Representatives in International Standard-Setting and Related Bodies

International standard-setting body	Number of LAC members	Total number of members
International Accounting Standards Board (IASB)	1	15
International Financial Reporting Interpretations Committee (IFRIC)	0	14
International Accounting Standards Committee (IASC) Foundation	1	22
IASB Standards Advisory Council (SAC)	2	38
International Ethics Standards Board for Accountants (IESBA)	0	18
International Auditing and Assurance Standards Board (IAASB)	0	18
International Auditing Education Standards Board (IAESB)	2	18
International Public Sector Accounting Standards Board (IPSASB)	0	18
Total	5	161

Source: Institutional Web sites (as of June 2009).

Establishing a Robust Standard-Setting Framework

Regardless of whether a country has decided to adopt IFRS, it needs a robust standard-setting framework to ensure that standards can be applied effectively. Creating such a framework involves four components: (a) providing sufficient legal backing for the framework, (b) establishing a multidisciplinary body in charge of issuing standards, (c) establishing a transparent and robust process for issuing standards, and (d) ensuring that market participants and regulators are adequately prepared.

Providing Sufficient Legal Backing for the Standard-Setting Framework

The standard-setting framework (including both the standards themselves and the standard-setting body) needs to be recognized and given adequate statutory authority. As chapter 2 explains, the law should define a set of accounting standards (commonly referred to as Generally Accepted Accounting Principles, or GAAP), as issued by a particular body, without detailing the actual standards that are to be followed by the reporting entities. The standard-setting body (for example, the accounting professional body or independent standard setter, depending on the country) would thereby be given the necessary legal authority to issue standards through appropriate instruments (resolutions, circulars, and the like). Most LAC countries have given legal backing to their local GAAP—and standard setters—in this manner. However, in some countries (for example, Paraguay), the law does not confer on any standard-setting body the authority to issue accounting standards, and GAAP in these countries have no legal definition. In other countries, accounting standards have been precisely defined in statute at a given point in time, without an administrative mechanism for updating them. As a result, these local GAAP have become incomplete and outdated. For example, Honduras's "15 First Honduran GAAP," issued in 1996, do not cover construction contracts, leases, employee benefits, deferred income taxes, and consolidation.

Establishing a Strong, Multidisciplinary Standard-Setting Body

Establishing a strong standard-setting body requires significant technical capacity and resources. First, the body must have competent staff with the right mix of skills and background. Second, it must be properly empowered by the national government to authoritatively set standards. And finally, it must have adequate funding to carry out its duties. Several LAC countries have not been able to fulfill these requirements, and their ability to regularly issue updated financial reporting standards suffers as a result.

In many LAC countries (Chile, Costa Rica, El Salvador, Panama, and Paraguay), the standard-setting bodies tend to be dominated by the accounting profession. While the profession has arguably the greatest understanding of the technical issues around accounting standards, it should not act alone in this endeavor. Accounting standards need to meet the needs of others, including businesses (which prepare financial statements), investors and creditors (who use financial statements to make business decisions), and regulators (who monitor and enforce compliance with the standards). Thus, to be effective, a standard-setting body should be multidisciplinary, with representation from the regulatory institutions of government, the private sector, and the academic community. It should be independent of the influence both of government and of the profession (UK Department of Trade and Industry 2003). Brazil's independent accounting standard setter, CPC, is an example of good practice in this regard (box 5.1).

Finally, many standard-setting bodies lack a sustainable source of funding. For example, in 2005, the independent audit oversight board and

---

Box 5.1

Brazil's CPC: Good Practice in Standard Setting

Brazil's Accounting Standards Committee (Comitê de Pronunciamentos Contábeis, or CPC) was established as an independent accounting standard-setting body in October 2005. CPC's membership includes representatives from (a) the Association of Listed Corporations, which represents preparers of financial statements; (b) the Association of Market Analysts, which represents investors; (c) BM&F BOVESPA, the stock exchange (a regulator); (d) CFC and IBRACON, both professional bodies representing accountants and auditors; and (e) the University of São Paulo's Accounting Research Institute, representing academia. Other regulators (such as the securities market and insurance sector supervisors, the central bank, and the tax authority) participate as observers. Stakeholders that are not represented directly in the CPC are able to participate in the standard-setting process by commenting on draft standards. All draft standards issued by CPC must be made public for at least 30 days before a final standard can be issued.

standard-setting body in El Salvador (described in box 3.3) had a technical staff of four and an administrative staff of five. It did not have a permanent executive, and its annual budget of US$110,000 was provided by the state. Members of the profession contributed their time on a *pro bono* basis. This level of staffing and funding is insufficient to effectively carry out the duties of a standard setter and independent audit oversight board.

Importance of a Robust and Transparent Standard-Setting Process

It is critical to have a transparent, well-defined process for issuing or adopting new standards or amendments. The process should include issuing exposure drafts and allowing ample time for public comment, so that the final standard reflects the needs of a wide group of stakeholders. Additionally, for first-time adoption of IFRS, the process should include (a) thoroughly analyzing each standard and interpretation to identify any difficulties it poses in relation to local laws, regulations, and circumstances; (b) conducting surveys of the accounting profession to assess the state of their knowledge of IFRS; and (c) requiring companies to test the application of IFRS on prior-year accounts, and monitoring those tests. There should be a public, detailed plan with a sequence of key activities (reviewing of standards, training of company accountants, "real-life" testing of IFRS). Such a process helps to ensure that companies, auditors, and regulators are adequately prepared to apply and enforce IFRS.

A few countries in the LAC region—Brazil, Chile, Mexico, and Uruguay—have established a robust process for adopting or issuing A&A standards, but others are struggling in this regard. For example, in Honduras, the law requiring the adoption of IFRS simply states that financial statements need to be prepared in accordance with IFRS, as adopted by the Technical Board (the Honduran standard setter), and it allows the Technical Board to make amendments to the standards, as needed. However, no implementing legislation was issued to detail the adoption process, and the Technical Board has not yet defined its strategy for adopting and implementing IFRS.[5] One example of a robust, albeit resource-intensive, standard-setting process is that of the European Union (box 5.2)

Ensuring that Market Participants and Regulators Are Adequately Prepared

Before issuing new or amended local standards, and particularly before transitioning to IFRS, it is important for the standard setter to take into consideration the capacity of preparers, auditors, and regulators. In some

Box 5.2

The European Union's Endorsement Process for IFRS

The EU required IFRS for the consolidated financial statements of listed companies in 2005, developing a robust process of "endorsement" to convert each IFRS into a binding standard in the EU.[a] However, the process requires significant time, technical capacity, and resources. After a standard has been issued by the IASB, it goes through the following steps (time estimates provided by the European Commission's Internal Market and Services Directorate General) (Madziar 2007; Gielen et al. 2007):

- European Commission (EC, the executive body of the European Union) receives technical endorsement advice from the European Financial Reporting Advisory Group (EFRAG) [2 months].
- EC receives an opinion from the Standards Advisory Review Group assessing whether EFRAG's technical advice is objective and well balanced [3 weeks].
- The standard is translated into the 23 official languages of the EU [3 weeks].
- The Accounting Regulatory Committee of the EC (ARC, which comprises representatives from all EU Member States) votes on whether to endorse the standard [2 months].
- The European Parliament votes to confirm the ARC's endorsement [3 months or more].
- If all these steps go well, the EC endorses the standard or interpretation and publishes it in the official journal.

All told, the average time between publication by the IASB and adoption of an endorsed standard by the EU has been about 8 to 10 months (Commission of the European Communities 2008). Since this process began, nearly all of IASB's standards have been endorsed as originally issued, except the two standards that deal with financial instruments (IAS 32 and 39) (Brackney and Witmer 2005).[b]

a. Australia, New Zealand, and other countries have also adopted similarly robust endorsement processes.

b. The major exceptions have been IAS 32 and IAS 39, which deal with financial instruments. The IASB and the EU could not resolve disagreement on certain small sections of IAS 39 (sections on fair value accounting and portfolio hedging). So the EU temporarily removed ("carved out") these sections from the EU's adoption review until a compromise standard can be devised and issued.

cases, significant capacity-building efforts may be required. Training for the adoption of IFRS could include the following kinds of activities:

- Developing a toolkit to help company controllers, external auditors, regulators, and users of the financial reporting familiarize themselves with IFRS;
- Updating university curricula and other relevant professional curricula to take into account the adoption of IFRS, and holding corresponding teacher-training workshops;
- Providing seminars, workshops, and other activities to help the private sector and government bodies understand and implement the changes; and
- Providing IFRS training sessions for the staff of the financial sector regulatory bodies.

The Chilean case offers an interesting look at the time and resources involved in IFRS adoption. Chile was the first large country in the LAC region to adopt IFRS in full, and its transition experience is particularly interesting because of the significance of its stock market (US$220 billion of market capitalization in February 2008). In late 2006, Chile's Superintendency of Securities and Insurance (SVS) decided to require securities issuers on its stock market to publish IFRS financial statements for reporting periods starting on or after January 1, 2009. Since issuing this requirement, SVS has (a) set up a clear and comprehensive section on IFRS on its Web site; (b) issued 10 circulars dealing with IFRS adoption; and (c) conducted two surveys of securities issuers to assess their degree of preparedness for implementation and identify possible difficulties and bottlenecks in the adoption process.[6] The staff of the accounting and research divisions of SVS have been working almost exclusively on preparing these regulations and reaching out to market participants. Yet, despite this intensive effort to ensure that securities issuers would be ready for the December 2009 deadline, SVS had to give issuers more time: it allowed issuers to present pro forma IFRS statements for FY09 (that is, without 2008 comparisons), and it extended by 30 days the deadline for submitting quarterly and year-end statements.[7] Clearly, having a strong and active regulatory body to move the process forward must be seen as a prerequisite to successful IFRS implementation; and the regulator must be proactive throughout the adoption process to anticipate and manage the risk of delays that any such project is prone to face.

Development institutions have been offering some assistance for such capacity-building efforts. For example, the Financial Sector Reform and Strengthening (FIRST) Initiative, a multidonor grant facility providing technical assistance to promote financial sector strengthening, has sponsored projects in four Latin American countries (Chile, El Salvador, Honduras, and Peru) that have directly or indirectly helped to build capacity for the transition to IFRS. In addition, the Inter-American Development Bank's Multilateral Investment Fund (MIF) sponsored projects in nine LAC countries to provide training toward the adoption of or convergence with IFRS.[8]

National GAAP: An Uncertain Future

Many countries—in LAC and around the world—continue to use local GAAP.[9] However, as larger countries, including the United States, transition to adoption of IFRS for listed companies, what will become of the notion of "local GAAP"? For now, they will most likely continue to exist, particularly for SMEs' financial reporting and for the legal entity financial statements of companies in general. Beyond the near term, however, this raises the issue of countries' willingness and ability to continue investing resources in updating these national standards to account for evolving business practices.

The versions of local GAAP that exist today differ significantly from IFRS (table 5.3). Having two sets of standards—IFRS for PIEs, and local

Table 5.3 Some Key Differences between National GAAP and IFRS

Countries that have retained national GAAP		IAS 32-39, IFRS 7: Financial Instruments	IAS 12: Income Taxes	IFRS 3: Business Combinations	IAS 19: Employee Benefits	IAS 14: Segment Reporting
Argentina	*		√	√		
Brazil	*	√	√	√		√
Chile	*	√	√	√	√	√
Colombia		√	√	√	√	√
Ecuador	*	√	√	√	√	
Mexico	*	√	√	√	√	√

Source: LAC ROSC A&A review.

Note: This table shows the most common departures from IFRS among local GAAP; a mark may represent anything from small differences to complete omission of a standard.

* Adopted (or soon to adopt) IFRS for listed companies.

GAAP for SMEs—may become a problem for these countries. If the differences in financial reporting standards for PIEs and non-PIEs are great, they may become a disincentive for companies to "scale up" their operations. One possible way to avoid such a problem may be the adoption of the recently issued IFRS for SMEs. Although there is some doubt as to whether these standards will be suitable for small companies, a simplified version of full IFRS—one that retains the main principles of the full standard—has the potential to serve LAC well.

IFRS for SMEs

The IFRS for SMEs project ought to draw the interest of LAC authorities.[10] The IFRS for SMEs were released as an exposure draft for public comment in February 2007, then formally issued in July 2009, as this book went to press. The lion's share of LAC enterprises are SMEs,[11] and there is an acknowledged need for a set of standards that fits their particular financial reporting requirements (IASB 2004). El Salvador has already formally recognized IFRS for SMEs; country authorities plan to mandate this new set of standards for nonregulated entities now that it has been released by the IASB. It is to be expected that most countries that have forgone national GAAP (Costa Rica, the Dominican Republic, El Salvador, Honduras, Nicaragua, Panama, Paraguay, Peru, Uruguay, and the English-speaking Caribbean countries) will seek to adopt IFRS for SMEs. One challenge on the horizon, therefore, is to determine which entities should apply which standards (that is, which companies are considered PIEs, which are considered SMEs, and which should be exempted altogether). Each country will need to define criteria and thresholds that are adapted to its particular environment.

IFRS in the Financial Sector

While IFRS adoption has been proceeding apace for listed companies, the results are decidedly mixed in the financial sector. Brazil is the only country to have officially adopted IFRS for the consolidated financial statements of banks and other financial institutions, with effective implementation in 2010. Other LAC countries have gradually moved toward IFRS adoption or convergence, but all of them still retain separate financial reporting standards for financial institutions. In most LAC countries, significant differences between IFRS and local standards remain with respect to the presentation of financial statements (IFRS 1), the valuation of loans and loan loss provisioning (IAS 39), securities investments (IAS 39), real estate assets (IAS 40), and insurance contracts (IFRS 4). Banking supervisors around the world, including in LAC, have expressed strong reservations about specific aspects of IFRS, in particular the fair value measurements of financial instruments required under IAS 39 (Tweedie 2004). In light of the significant advances banking supervisors have achieved in prudential supervision in LAC, it is understandable that they are wary of transitioning to IFRS, a system of financial reporting that differs significantly from prudential reporting with regard to risk perception, risk measurement, and presentation. In the context of the current global financial crisis, the banking supervisors' cautious (if not reluctant) approach to IFRS convergence is understandable and seems justified.

However, there are clear benefits in adopting IFRS for the financial sector. For one, completely separate prudential and financial reporting is costly, particularly since many financial institutions are listed and must therefore follow IFRS in several countries. Furthermore, separating financial from prudential reporting can result in internal control risks and behavioral risks (Schilder 2006). In addition, LAC banks are undergoing a transformation due to waves of acquisitions by European and U.S. banks (examples abound in virtually all countries except República Bolivariana de Venezuela); this phenomenon has had the effect of integrating LAC banks (even many of those that are not acquired) into the world banking system. One of the interesting aspects of integration is the move toward a more proactive approach to risk management[12] that is consistent with, and needed for, implementing IFRS.

The differences between IFRS and prudential reporting are not insurmountable, and the LAC region may draw on the lessons learned from the EU's adoption of IFRS in 2005. European banking regulators have been using several tools to bridge the gap between prudential and financial reporting under IFRS. For example, they may use prudential filters, which adjust financial reporting to separate issues relating to "real" or economic aspects, as opposed to "artificial" aspects, relating to accounting treatment (for example, banking supervisors often do not recognize goodwill, as it is not considered to be a reliable component of a bank's equity). In addition, banking supervisors often give prudential guidance—that is, they accept financial reporting on the condition that supervised institutions be subject to robust risk management systems, consistent with prudential norms. Finally, since IFRS offers much flexibility with regard to the presentation of financial statements, banking supervisors may require the use of prudential reporting templates to achieve more consistent reporting by banks (Schilder 2006).

Adoption of International Standards on Auditing in LAC

While this chapter has not separately discussed International Standards on Auditing (ISA), much of what has been written about international accounting standards applies to auditing. The Dominican Republic, El Salvador, Peru, and Honduras legally require all statutory auditors to apply ISA when carrying out financial statement audits (table 5.4).

In auditing, as in accounting, a familiar pattern emerges: the largest countries retain their own local auditing standards while the smaller countries adopt ISA for all statutory audits or audits of PIEs. Larger countries have their own audit standards (Generally Accepted Auditing Standards, or GAAS) that typically fall short of international standards in several aspects. Each ROSC analyzes the quality of any local auditing standards against ISA; the most common departures from ISA the ROSCs have found arise from the fact that many local auditing standards do not specify as explicitly as ISA 260 the types of issues that the auditor should communicate at the outset of an engagement to those charged with cor-

Table 5.4 Statutory Adoption of International Standards on Auditing (ISA)

Country	All companies	Banking sector	Listed companies	Non-bank financial institutions
Argentina				
Brazil		√		
Chile				
Colombia				
Dominican Republic	√	√	√	√
Ecuador		√		√
El Salvador	√	√	√	√
Haiti		√	n.a.	
Honduras	√	√	√	√
Jamaica		√	√	√
Mexico				
OECS		√		
Panama	√	√	√	√
Paraguay				
Peru	√	√	√	√
Uruguay			√	

Source: LAC ROSC A&A review.

Note: n.a. – Not applicable.

porate governance (for example, the scope, the timing, and what constitutes materiality in the audit). In addition, local auditing standards sometimes do not cover the auditor's responsibility to consider fraud during the audit of financial statements.

Large international audit networks generally require more stringent standards on audits than the local law. In 2002, these audit networks formed the Forum of Firms (FoF), an organization of international firms that perform audits of financial statements that are or may be used across national borders ("transnational audits"). Members of the FoF agreed to meet certain requirements, detailed in the FoF Constitution: a commitment to the FoF "Quality Standard," which requires member firms to adhere to ISA in addition to relevant national auditing standards; and to maintain internal quality control systems to ensure compliance with minimum auditing, ethics, and training requirements.[13]

Most of the statutory audits of PIEs in the LAC region are carried out by member firms of one of the international audit networks, which are required by internal quality control rules to follow ISA. In theory, the local accountancy professional bodies that are members of IFAC are required by IFAC's Statements of Membership Obligations (IFAC 2006) to adopt ISA and enforce them among their membership (although, as discussed in chapters 3 and 6, the professional bodies rarely enforce such requirements). The profession, to enhance its reputation for quality, should take the lead in adopting ISA. Absent such adoption, at a minimum, the securities market and financial sector regulators should enact ISA in their regulations and require that all statutory auditors of entities under their purview adhere to international standards.

Fortunately, the adoption and application of ISA is much less challenging to attain than IFRS because implementing the change involves only the members of the A&A profession, rather than the entire business community—and the member firms of the international audit networks already require ISA. There is already momentum to adopt ISA. The most important remaining challenge is enforcing compliance.

Conclusion

The global financial crisis has underscored the need to continue to move toward sound international A&A standards. Indeed, the G-20, meeting in April 2009 during the most severe global financial and economic crisis in at least a generation, called on accounting standard setters "to make significant progress towards a single set of high quality global accounting standards" (Group of 20 2009, 6). Their "Declaration on Strengthening the Financial System" also called for the World Bank to continue evaluating progress toward implementing IFRS and ISA, among other key international standards and codes, to help maintain financial stability and enhance the openness and transparency of the financial sector.

The stability and growth that most of LAC's economies experienced during the 2000s allowed space and flexibility to begin to implement international standards. Today, most LAC countries have adopted or committed to adopt IFRS for listed companies, and most have adopted ISA for the financial statement audits of PIEs. This represents a shift for most of the larger countries of the region, which had previously chosen to adapt international standards to their national requirements. Except for Brazil, countries have not adopted IFRS for banks and other financial institutions. Brazil's experience in the coming years will likely have a significant influence on other regional policy makers, as they determine the appropriateness of international standards for their financial sectors. Effective implementation is difficult—arguably more so than adoption— and it will be critical for national standard setters, regulators, and the profession to continue to work together to develop realistic timelines and procedures to facilitate a smooth transition to international standards.

A significant challenge is determining the appropriate requirements for SMEs, which are very important to LAC's economic development. IFRS and full-scale audits are not appropriate for most companies on the smaller end of the spectrum. It will be important for policy makers to give careful consideration to the requirements they impose on these companies, and to the size thresholds that determine the applicable requirements. IASB's IFRS for SMEs hold promise as an approach to solving the problem, and many countries in LAC that currently require full IFRS for all companies will adopt IFRS for SMEs now that they have been released. This looming challenge can also be viewed as an opportunity for the region's A&A standard setters to collaborate on areas of common concern, such as defining common measures and thresholds of scale for SMEs, adopting a common Spanish-language translation of IFRS for SMEs, developing a less intensive audit model for SMEs, and producing joint comments on exposure drafts of international standards.

Notes

1. It is often said that smaller countries "adopt" IFRS, while large countries "adapt" them, meaning that they modify the standards to fit local needs.

2. In Chile, the requirement only applies to companies with a free float greater than or equal to 25 percent. For more information on Mexico, see http://www.cnbv.gob.mx/recursos/056_Adopcion_IFRS_english.pdf.

3. For a timeline of IFRS revisions and other IASB projects, see Deloitte's IAS+ Web site at http://www.iasplus.com/agenda/agenda.htm.

4. ROSC A&A for El Salvador, p. 12.

5. ROSC A&A for Honduras, p. 37.

6. Superintendencia de Valores y Seguros de Chile, IFRS Update, http://www.svs.cl/sitio/mercados/ifrs_aldia.php?mercado=S.

7. SVS Circular 427, Dec. 2007, and SVS Circular 473, Sept. 2008.

8. See the MIF Accounting & Auditing Standards Cluster home page at http://www.iadb.org/mif/subtopic.cfm?lang=en&subtopic=aust&topic=fcd.

9. For example, the Mexican financial reporting standard setter, CINIF, lists among its Web site's "Articles of Interest" a 1959 speech advocating the creation of a "Mexican School" of Accounting (Galeazzi Mora 1959).

10. According to IASB, the objective of this project is "to develop an IFRS expressly designed to meet the financial reporting needs of entities that (a) do not have public accountability and (b) publish general purpose financial statements for external users. Examples of such external users include owners who are not involved in managing the business, existing and potential creditors, and credit rating agencies. The IFRS for SMEs will be derived from full IFRSs with appropriate modifications based on the needs of users of private entity financial statements and cost-benefit considerations" (http://www.iasb.org).

11. Due to varying definitions of the term and a high degree of informality, concrete statistics for Latin American SMEs are difficult to find, but one Inter-American Development Bank study estimates that 80 percent of employment in the region is generated by microenterprises and SMEs (Márquez, Barreix, and Villela 2007).

12. That is, a system of management emphasizing risk, with the accompanying infrastructure of internal controls and governance mechanisms.

13. For more on the history and activities of the Forum of Firms, see http://www.ifac.org/Forum_of_Firms.

CHAPTER 6

Ensuring Compliance with Accounting and Auditing Standards

The Challenges of Effective Enforcement

Throughout the discussions in this book—the essential accounting and auditing (A&A) statutory framework, the adoption of international standards, and upholding the reputation of the accounting profession—we have touched on the need for strong enforcement. It goes without saying that the quality of the laws and standards is virtually irrelevant when companies and individuals generally do not comply with them, and the laws are weakly or unevenly enforced.[1]

The Reports on the Observance of Standards and Codes, Accounting and Auditing (ROSC A&A) reviews have shown that noncompliance with A&A rules is an issue in nearly every country in the Latin America and Caribbean (LAC) region, particularly in nonfinancial sectors. The weakness in compliance affects other areas of the A&A environment, such as the reputation of the profession, the statutory framework that governs corporate financial reporting, and sector-specific regulation of public interest entities (PIEs) and other companies. This chapter describes some of the root causes of the lack of compliance with A&A standards in the region, and the barriers to effective enforcement.

Few Incentives to Produce Reliable Financial Information

There are few incentives—and several disincentives—for companies to follow applicable A&A rules. The ROSC reports most frequently cite the following reasons for noncompliance: (a) the fact that banks and other lenders generally do not engage in financial statement lending; (b) the absence of a requirement for large, nonlisted companies to publish their financial statements; (c) a lack of effective penalties for noncompliance; (d) the cultural legacy of family-run businesses; and (e) a lack of capacity or resources to prepare compliant financial reports.

Use of Financial Information by Creditors and Investors in Private Entities

In LAC countries, unlike in many Organisation for Economic Co-operation and Development (OECD) countries, investors, banks, and other lenders rarely use financial statements to determine creditworthiness (OECD 2006). Instead, family or personal ties, or high collateral requirements, replace financial information and market discipline in determining to whom lenders extend credit (a notable exception is on the stock markets). For example, a study of Latin American banks found that risk assessment of small and medium enterprises (SMEs) using credit-scoring techniques driven by financial data is uncommon in the region (FELABAN, FOMIN, and D'Alessio Irol 2004), while banks in OECD countries have widely adopted the practice (OECD 2006). Instead, 70 percent of LAC banks reported making their SME lending decisions on a "case by case" basis (FELABAN, FOMIN, and D'Alessio Irol 2004). Furthermore, the ROSC A&A assessments frequently report that lenders and other users have substantially less confidence in the financial statements of companies outside of supervised sectors. There is thus little demand for high-quality financial statements from the private sector, outside of listed companies.

Financial Statement Publishing Requirements for Large, Nonlisted Companies

The fact that, except in Brazil and Mexico, large, nonlisted companies are not often required to publish their financial statements removes another incentive to prepare financial reports in accordance with the prevailing standards.[2] Other countries, including Argentina and Uruguay, require companies to deposit their financial statements with a company registrar, where third parties have access to them; yet these registrars are not equipped to review the financial statements for adherence to financial reporting standards, so there is no assurance of the statements' reliability. Moreover, at times access to these financial statements is difficult (in Argentina, the registrar requires three to six months to provide a copy of paper-based financial statements, or 15 to 30 days if urgent). Thus, the registrars' usefulness to third parties is limited. In the future, technology may resolve some of these difficulties and help registrars achieve their potential as storehouses of financial data. For example, Internet-based transmission and storage of financial statements might alleviate some of the difficulties and expense of storing and retrieving this information. Timely access to sound financial data would significantly reduce the information asymmetries that banks report as an obstacle to their lending to private entities.

Penalties for Noncompliance

The threat of penalties for noncompliance is a common incentive to comply with the rules. Yet most LAC businesses that fail to follow applicable A&A rules and standards are unlikely to face sanctions, even where such sanctions exist. Regulators vary in capabilities across countries and sectors, but they generally lack the resources and qualified staff they need to effectively carry out their mandate. In particular, enforcement for nonregulated entities is virtually nonexistent. Furthermore, sanctions are rarely imposed on businesses in virtually any sector. (The contours of enforcement capabilities and sanctioning regimes are described in greater detail later in this section.)

Lack of Transparency

Another reason that LAC companies may not comply with financial reporting rules is related to the region's business traditions. Many companies have traditionally been closely held within families and are not accustomed to disclosing financial information (OECD 2003); revealing the wealth of a family-owned company is akin to revealing the family's personal wealth. The traditional predominance of family-owned businesses may contribute to an ingrained culture of nontransparency: out of custom, these companies may avoid disclosure even after ownership becomes more widespread, and they frequently set the tone for the business community at large (Chiraz, Trabelsi, and Gettler Summa 2007). This passage from the Honduras ROSC report describes several issues related to family ownership that help explain the lack of interest in complying with financial reporting rules:

> Honduran companies are still largely family-owned and the business community generally sees limited interest in external financial reporting. In fact, many businesses view financial reporting as a possible threat to business

secrets, as well as to their personal safety, as they believe that disclosing financial information about their companies would expose them to significant risk of kidnappings and other crimes.

Lack of Capacity or Resources

Finally, many companies are reluctant to comply with accounting requirements, particularly international standards, because they lack capacity or resources to do so. It is quite difficult to comply with IFRS, and even with national accounting standards. Ensuring compliance requires a sufficient and adequately skilled staff (for example, professional accountants and people with an auditing background). Companies may not give priority to hiring more staff members with the experience and qualifications to bring the business into compliance with financial reporting standards.

Enforcement of Financial Reporting Requirements

This section examines the enforcement of financial reporting requirements for regulated entities and nonregulated entities (nonlisted, nonfinancial companies), as well as of professional standards for the accounting profession.

Enforcement for Regulated Entities

Regulatory agencies have generally adequate statutory enforcement powers. They are usually empowered to conduct inspections of companies under their purview and of their independent auditors (for example, to request working papers and other supporting documents). Ideally, they should thoroughly and systematically review financial statements (using relevant sampling techniques) to identify departures from financial reporting rules, and should request clarifications when necessary. In addition, specific events—such as a qualified audit report, late filing, public offering (in the case of a listed company), or investor complaint—should trigger an investigation. Regulators are generally empowered to impose administrative sanctions for noncompliance. However, they often lack staff with the required skills and experience—in particular, accounting expertise—to ensure that financial reporting requirements are being met. Although some countries (Brazil, for example) enforce financial reporting rules, the scarcity of qualified accountants with expertise in International Financial Reporting Standards (IFRS) and International Standards on Accounting (ISA) means that compliance with applicable accounting rules is uneven. The ROSC financial statement reviews show significant departures from applicable financial reporting standards (box 6.1).

Box 6.1

Compliance with Applicable Accounting Standards: Evidence from the ROSC A&A

According to an analysis of the ROSC reports, the following are the most common departures from prevailing accounting standards (local GAAP or IFRS, depending on local requirements):

Taxation. Accounting standards for general-purpose financial statements differ in important ways from the standards used for the purposes of taxation. When companies do not clearly differentiate between these two different sets of rules, confusion ensues. In many cases, disclosures were insufficient for the ROSC A&A reviewers to gain a proper understanding of the company's tax position.[a] Another common problem is the failure to apply deferred taxes; this issue is particularly important for companies that revalue their property, as failing to recognize the implicit tax effect of a revaluation leads to inflating the equity value of the company.

Segment Reporting. Segment information is an important part of adequate disclosure of a company's business, as it helps users understand the company's performance and cash flows, and therefore make more informed decisions overall. Even in countries where disclosure of segment information is required under IFRS (IAS 14, now superseded by IFRS 8) or national standards, it is fairly common for notes to lack disclosures regarding a company's business segments.

Financial Instruments. Inexact information about the significance and category of financial instruments was common. Disclosures on the nature of and exposure to risks (credit, liquidity, and market) were generally lacking. Some countries that have adopted IFRS requirements regarding financial instruments have postponed or carved out exceptions to the requirements relating to fair value and the calculation of effective interest rates. And where companies do use fair value to account for their financial instruments, they often do not adequately disclose the calculations that led them to their valuations.

Provisions, Contingent Liabilities, and Contingent Assets. If this information is not disclosed properly, it is very difficult for an investor to assess the size of a company's total potential liabilities and assets and make a robust analysis of the company's financial condition. Yet ROSC A&A reports in several countries observed that companies commonly failed to provide information concerning restricted fixed assets that had been pledged as security, or the existence of contingent liabilities and provisions.

(Box continues on the following page.)

Box 6.1 (*continued*)

Related-Party Disclosures. Disclosures of related-party relationships and transactions are particularly sensitive for the protection of investors and, to a lesser degree, lenders. They represent an essential feature of a good corporate governance framework. Related-party transactions present a heightened risk of conflicts of interest or improper valuation (or the perception or appearance thereof).[b] The reviews found that in several countries the disclosure of related-party relationships and transactions was broadly incomplete, especially with respect to the pricing policies and other information necessary to understand such transactions.

The fact that the problems or weaknesses in the financial statements reviewed for the ROSCs were not detected or sanctioned by the regulatory bodies charged with enforcing the standards is further testament to the need to strengthen enforcement of accounting standards.

a. For example, the ROSC review in Uruguay found that a company had recorded as a profit a deferred tax benefit related to the utilization of tax losses carried forward from prior years. This treatment had the effect of bringing the net income for the period from a loss to a profit. Considering its material impact on the net income, this item should have been highlighted in the notes, and the rationale for the way it was accounted for should have been explained.

b. A notorious example is Enron, which used related-party transactions with "special-purpose entities" to distort the company's financial statements and artificially inflate the perceived value of the company.

Banks. Of the regulated sectors, the banking sector tends to be subject to the most stringent enforcement, as banking supervisors consistently have more human and financial resources than regulators of other sectors. This seems only natural in countries where financial sector instability is relatively common and where there are limited mechanisms for market discipline (given the weakness of the financial reporting regime). Almost all banking supervisors in LAC are structured as a two-tier system. One tier, the on-site supervision department, generally conducts an annual on-site inspection of banks. In almost all countries, the second tier—the off-site supervision department—is linked to banks via an online system, through which it is able to check compliance with requirements (mostly prudential requirements) on a real-time basis.

Nonbank Financial Institutions. Overall, the ROSC reports have observed more limited oversight capabilities for nonbank financial institutions than for banks. Nonbank financial institutions include insurance companies, pension funds, investment societies, credit cooperatives, and so on, and each of these sectors tends to be supervised by a separate regulatory body. Some countries have combined the enforcement functions for all financial institutions (including banks, pension funds, insurance companies, and other nonbank entities) into one regulatory body. This practice promotes coordination among regulators and generally strengthens oversight. (Box 6.2 describes an example of subregional coordination in this area.)

Listed Companies. The human and financial resources for enforcing stock markets track closely with the significance of the stock market: the

---

Box 6.2

The Organisation of Eastern Caribbean States (OECS): A Lesson in Cooperation

Although each of the independent OECS countries has its own unique history and tradition, the erosion of trade preferences and other globalizing forces have pushed all of them to work together to integrate their economies. Business and government leaders agree that they must pool scarce human and other resources to remain competitive, and the OECS has made significant strides toward greater subregional integration.

Sound, universal financial reporting standards such as IFRS are a key piece of the puzzle. A number of uniform acts regulating the financial services industry have been enacted (Banking Act) or drafted (Insurance and Co-operative Societies Acts) to harmonize the legislation of member countries. As part of a move toward regulatory reform of the nonbank financial sector, the Eastern Caribbean Central Bank has spearheaded an initiative to establish standalone Single Regulatory Units, which would regulate and supervise all nonbank financial institutions in each of the member countries. The continued development of the region's money and capital markets is another important aspect of the subregion's development strategy. In 2001 a subregional securities market, the Eastern Caribbean Stock Exchange, was established, regulated by the Eastern Caribbean Securities Regulatory Commission.

regulators of the Brazilian, Chilean, and Panamanian stock markets are the best equipped to oversee those relatively larger exchanges. For countries whose stock markets have only a few listed companies (for example, Paraguay or the OECS), the regulators of these exchanges have more limited resources; they lack the critical mass of resources necessary to hire the competent staff and put into place the mechanisms for a well-functioning and well-regulated stock market. Reaching this critical mass is a crucial yet difficult challenge for these smaller stock markets, as companies seek out larger stock markets upon which to list when possible, and many investors prefer to invest on more established exchanges. Of course, one of the factors for the relative lack of investor interest in these smaller capital markets is likely the limited capabilities of the regulators (de la Torre and Schmukler 2007; Friedman and Grose 2006). Strong enforcement mechanisms are therefore an important piece of the puzzle.

State-Owned Enterprises. In most cases, state-owned enterprises (SOEs) are under the supervision of supreme audit institutions (SAIs). Yet SAIs are typically charged mainly with overseeing nonenterprise branches of government—for example, monitoring over-budget execution of government programs (OECD 2005)—and they commonly lack the resources and staff capacity to conduct annual audits of SOEs in accordance with ISA or other internationally accepted auditing standards for the private sector (Dye and Stapenhurst 1998). Although it is widely believed that SOEs should be subject to the same financial reporting regime as companies in the private sector,[3] SAIs and public financial management laws do not normally distinguish between A&A standards for the general public sector and for SOEs.

Enforcement for Nonregulated Entities
Most countries have no body that is responsible for ensuring that nonregulated companies comply with financial reporting requirements. In countries that do have such a body (for example, Colombia, Ecuador, El Salvador), enforcement of financial reporting requirements for nonregulated companies is generally done reactively—that is, in response to a complaint from a user. In addition, several countries (for example, Argentina, the OECS, and Uruguay) require nonlisted companies to deposit their financial statements with a company registrar, which third parties may access; but since the registrars do not review these financial statements, there is no assurance of their reliability. For countries that do

not have an enforcement system in place, requiring an external audit of large, nonlisted companies would be one way to "enforce" financial reporting requirements without creating an extensive enforcement framework.

Enforcement of Auditing and Professional Standards

Given the disincentives for LAC companies to comply with prevailing standards and regulations, and the capacity constraints and weaknesses among those charged with enforcing accounting and financial reporting rules, the independent audit takes on even greater importance. In most cases, the auditor is the only external reviewer of corporate financial statements with both the expertise to detect problems and the authority to compel modifications. It is therefore essential that auditors adhere to strict auditing and professional standards. If outside users are to trust corporate financial statements, their confidence will probably come in large part from the seal of quality that a clean audit opinion from a reputable auditor represents.

A few accountancy bodies have instituted peer review systems to verify compliance with professional standards. Among the countries reviewed in the ROSC A&A program, only three professional accountancy bodies had put into place a quality assurance mechanism for auditors or accountants. Under Brazil's CFC peer review system, auditors must have their work reviewed by a disinterested fellow auditor. In El Salvador, the Accounting and Auditing Professional Oversight Board (Consejo de Vigilancia de la Profesión de Contaduría Pública y de Auditoría, or CVPCPA) began piloting a small-scale peer review system in 2005. And in Jamaica, the Institute of Chartered Accountants of Jamaica (ICAJ) Accounting Standards Committee reviews the financial statements of all listed companies and reports the findings to the auditor and to the ICAJ Council in summary form. It also reports significant compliance issues to the Auditing Practice Committee of ICAJ and, if appropriate, the Disciplinary Committee. However, except for these efforts, most professional accountancy bodies do not attempt to enforce quality standards for auditors. This runs counter to Statement of Membership Obligations 1 of the International Federation of Accountants (IFAC), which stipulates that IFAC member bodies should ensure that "a mandatory quality assurance review program is in place for those of its members performing audits of financial statements of, as a minimum, listed entities." (Quality assurance is defined as a review to determine whether auditors have adhered to professional standards and regulatory and legal requirements in performing engagements; see IFAC 2006).

Global audit networks have their own quality assurance mechanisms in place, but these mechanisms are not transparent, and regulators and financial statement users cannot rely on them. As a 2004 World Bank publication on the lessons learned from the global ROSC A&A program noted,

> Despite the expectations that flow from the use of their global brands, the ROSC results and audit failures over recent years in several jurisdictions would suggest that international audit firm networks do not deliver consistent, high-quality audit services across the globe. (Hegarty, Gielen, and Hirata Barros 2004, 19)

The member firms of the international audit firm networks are owned, operated, and regulated at the national, not the international, level. In spite of the implied promise of quality in the international networks' brand names, there is not a clear mechanism to enforce quality standards internationally.

As the old saying goes, and as many headlines asked in the wake of Enron and other corporate scandals: *Who will guard the guardians?* The United States and many other OECD countries provided a robust answer by establishing independent auditor oversight bodies (described in chapter 3), supplanting the old system of professional self-regulation. These bodies register qualified auditors, set standards of professional and ethical conduct, and enforce the standards through inspections or other mechanisms. This development has been very well received among the investment community worldwide and the users of financial statements in general. However, these oversight institutions remain rare in LAC. Other mechanisms to foster audit quality (such as mandatory education requirements, professional examination requirements, and continuing professional development requirements) are unevenly applied and, in any event, are insufficient to ensure an acceptable level of quality. In the absence of independent oversight, enforcement of auditing and ethical standards is left to the professional bodies themselves, under the traditional self-regulation arrangements—which, as the ROSC program has found, are unsatisfactory (box 6.3).

Disciplinary Regimes

One deterrent that is missing from most regulatory regimes in the region is credible and public sanctions. Of 17 countries surveyed, only 5

Box 6.3

Compliance with Applicable Auditing Standards: Evidence from the ROSC A&A

Some of the most commonly observed problems with audit reports include the following:

Absence of required qualifications in the opinions on financial statements. The compliance problems detected in the ROSC reviews should often have led to qualified or adverse audit opinions, but they rarely did. In fact, many of the problems were detected in financial reports with "clean" or unqualified audit opinions. Thus, users may question the quality of the audit in general—and, by extension, of all independent audits.

Inconsistencies in the form of the audit report or the wording of qualifications. Statutory audit reports are official certificates and, when prepared under ISA, should strictly follow the wording prescribed in ISA 700, The Auditor's Report on Financial Statements. One of the fundamental principles of ISA or other audit standards is the need for standardization and consistency in the wording of audit reports to ensure they are easily, clearly, and unambiguously understood. Similarly, it is important that, when an audit raises a concern about a financial statement, it uses the correct and complete terminology prescribed by ISA or the prevailing audit standard. To illustrate, the Chile ROSC describes a case in which the audit report described a "scope limitation," which was not technically a scope limitation, and which actually should have led to a qualified audit opinion.[a] Using nonstandard and sometimes ambiguous language leaves room for doubt and confusion among the users of audited financial statements, undermining the overall usefulness of the audit report.

Unclear or ambiguous language regarding the accounting or auditing standard used (for example, "GAAP" or "GAAS," without further clarification). It is important to define clearly the audit and accounting frameworks under which the audit is carried out, so that knowledgeable users have a basis for evaluating and comparing the financial information it contains. In some countries, auditors used the term "Generally Accepted Auditing Standards" when no such standards are published or spelled out in law, or they issued a clean audit opinion on financial statements that are said to be prepared under GAAP, when these standards are similarly unclear. Users wishing to compare these financial statements with others prepared under IFRS and audited using ISA may be at a loss.

(Box continues on the following page.)

Box 6.3 (*continued*)

Financial statements are too often prepared by the external auditors, not by the companies themselves. Where there is a dearth of qualified accountants, or during a transition to an unfamiliar new standard like IFRS, external auditors can help accountants employed by companies learn how to deal with the new requirements. However, having the auditors prepare, rather than review, the financial statements limits the company's concerns for the quality of its financial statements, leads to a lower level of assurance on the quality of these statements, and limits the independence of external auditors when auditing the company's financial statements. Moreover, this practice runs contrary to IFAC's Code of Ethics and most local codes of ethics as well.

a. See Chile A&A ROSC, Section IV, available at http://www.worldbank.org/ifa/rosc_aa_chl.pdf.

(Argentina, Brazil, Chile, Colombia, and Panama) have banking supervisors that publish their sanctions on their Web sites. Fewer than half of all regulatory entities in any sector publish their sanctions. Sanctions that are not publicized lose much of their deterrent effect. Moreover, public sanctions act as a "report card" on the work of the regulator: it is very difficult to assess whether a regulator is actively enforcing requirements if there is no public information on sanctions (including warnings, requests for additional information, and so on).

When sanctions are published, the information disclosed is often incomplete, lacking important details (for example, a brief summary of the requirement violated) that would give a better understanding to users not familiar with specific articles of the applicable regulation. It is important for third parties to know why a particular sanction was imposed if they are to judge the reliability of the financial reports. It is also important to know the magnitude of the sanction, which is not always noted. For example, most sanctions seem to be based on questions of form (such as on-time submission), rather than on the content and accuracy of the financial reports themselves or the conduct of the statutory audit. However, in one country, the regulator's Web site mentions that it issued a warning (*amonestación*) to a major international bank, but it does not indicate the reason for the warning. On the same day, the regulator fined a money-transfer company nearly US$500,000 for "Failure to comply with Chapter XI, Title 1 of the Basic Judicial Circular of 1996." The Web site does not indicate that this section of regulations refers to measures to prevent money laundering and terrorist financing, and it does not specify which parts of the regulation were violated. This fine was subsequently reduced to approximately US$100,000 without a published explanation. Such lack of contextual detail may be confusing to third-party users.

The Web site of the Chilean Securities and Insurance Superintendency (SVS) is an example of good practice in this respect. The list of sanctions imposed on companies is easily accessible, comprehensive, and user friendly. Users can search by category of supervised entities (including by external auditors) and for any desired timeframe between 2001 and 2008. The full decision memo—which contains details about the laws or regulations violated, the amount of any fine, and the justification for the fine—is also available. SVS also makes its management reports available online, allowing users to access aggregated statistics about sanctions imposed on both insurance and securities markets. Unfortunately, few countries' regulatory bodies have the resources to provide this level of information on their sanctions.

All these weaknesses are often compounded by a fragmented regulatory framework—that is, too many different agencies to review financial statements, when one would be sufficient (this problem is discussed in greater detail in chapter 2).

Conclusion

Countries must effectively enforce A&A standards if they are to realize the benefits of high-quality financial information. Even if countries construct a strong statutory framework and adopt best-practice standards, they will see few actual improvements unless they commit resources to credible enforcement measures. The ROSC A&A reports frequently recommend that country authorities adopt a less ambitious A&A regime and enforce it well, rather than unrealistically seeking adherence to complex international standards when they are not in a position to ensure compliance. Weak enforcement undermines the rule of law itself, as companies and individuals grow accustomed to the laws' going unenforced. In essence, sound enforcement practices are the cement that holds together the other building blocks of a strong A&A structure.

Notes

1. For the purposes of this section, we use "enforcement" in its broader sense of "compelling the fulfillment of (a law, demand, obligation)," rather than the narrow sense of sanctions and other direct actions to ensure compliance ("Enforcement," Oxford English Dictionary, Oxford University Press, 2008).

2. Mexico has a universal requirement for all companies to publish their financial statements. In Brazil, this requirement is applicable only to corporations.

3. The "Guidelines on Corporate Governance in State-Owned Enterprises" published in 2005 by the OECD recommend that SOEs "be subject to the same high quality accounting and auditing standards as listed companies," and that they be audited by an independent external auditor. These are aside from the requirements related to the preparation of public-sector consolidated accounts, which involve specific presentation and the use of a specific chart of accounts compatible with the government accounting plan. These additional requirements should not impede SOEs from preparing financial statements in the same way as if they operated as private-sector companies.

CHAPTER 7

A Roadmap for Reform

A strong corporate financial reporting framework rests on three pillars: (a) setting adequate requirements; (b) ensuring capacity to implement these requirements, especially with regard to the accounting profession; and (c) ensuring an appropriate level of compliance through enforcement (figure 7.1). Financial reporting requirements (including laws, regulations, mandatory standards, and other rules) need to be in line with business needs, the capacity of companies to follow the requirements, and the capacity of regulators to enforce them. Requirements that are too lax reduce public trust in financial reporting and do not enhance the business environment; requirements that are overly stringent may be unenforceable because practitioners and regulators lack capacity. All involved parties—including preparers and users of financial statements, auditors, regulators, and academics—need to understand what the rules are and how to apply them. Finally, financial regulators (for example, banking, insurance, and securities market regulators) need to enforce the rules evenhandedly and consistently.

Strengthening each pillar entails a set of reforms that range in complexity and urgency. Since every country is at a unique point in the reform process, each one necessarily has different reform priorities. Throughout the preceding chapters, this book has provided various suggestions for reform.

Figure 7.1 Foundations of a Sound Corporate Financial Reporting Framework

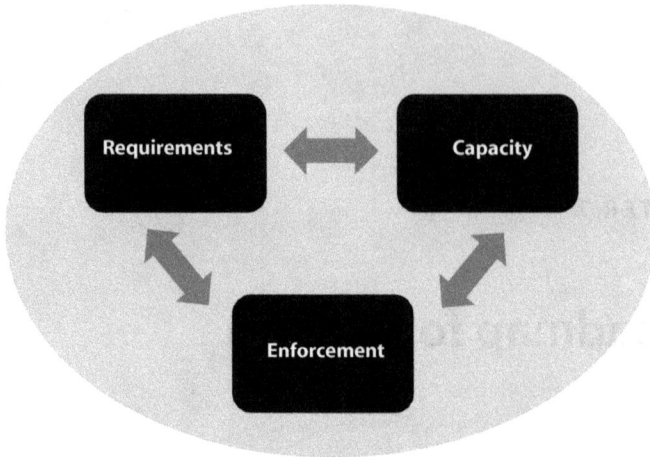

Source: Authors.

The purpose of this chapter is not to set forth a comprehensive, standard set of priorities for all countries in Latin America and the Caribbean (LAC), but rather to illustrate which reforms within each pillar are most pressing in the region as a whole. Individual countries are urged to develop a comprehensive Country Action Plan to implement the Reports on the Observance of Standards and Codes (ROSC) policy recommendations in a way that is consistent with their specific private and financial sector development reform needs. Appendix D provides specific guidance in this regard.

Pillar 1: Setting Adequate Requirements

As a rule, the higher the level of public responsibility, the more stringent the requirements should be. Statutory requirements should be lighter for companies with lower levels of public responsibility. Different types and sizes of companies should receive different treatment under the law—including different accounting, financial reporting, and audit obligations—depending on their level of responsibility to the public (figure 7.2). Several factors help determine a company's level of responsibility,[1] including whether it:

- Receives funds from the public in a fiduciary capacity (for example, banks and insurance companies)

Figure 7.2 "Right-Sizing" the Rules

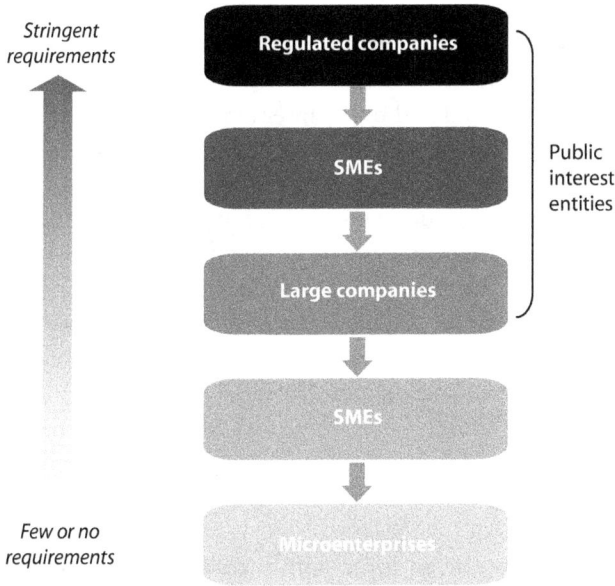

Source: Authors.

- Issues securities that are publicly traded (that is, is a listed company)
- Provides essential public services, such as public utilities, or is owned by the state
- Operates in strategic sectors (for example, defense) or is a monopoly
- Carries significant levels of debt
- Is economically significant to the country as a whole.

Most countries in the LAC region have put in place adequate rules for regulated companies (that is, financial institutions and listed companies), in line with good international practice. For example, a majority of LAC countries have already adopted International Financial Reporting Standards (IFRS) for corporate financial reporting and International Standards on Auditing (ISA) for statutory audits; and Argentina, Brazil, Chile, and Mexico are set to implement IFRS in 2010–11 for listed companies. In addition, most countries require that the financial statements of such regulated companies be audited and made available to the public.

However, the requirements for other public interest entities (PIEs), particularly state-owned enterprises (SOEs), generally are not stringent enough. In most LAC countries, SOEs are not required to follow the same accounting, audit, reporting, and internal control rules as private companies. Instead, they are generally required to follow public sector accounting and audit rules, which are not suited for commercial entities.

Across the region, small and medium enterprises (SMEs) tend to face statutory requirements that are too demanding. Some countries require even SMEs to conform to IFRS. IFRS were not designed for SMEs, and requiring compliance with such a complex set of standards is likely to create difficulties for these entities, without bringing obvious corresponding benefits. Also, some countries require SMEs to undergo an annual external audit. Requirements to undergo statutory audits or make financial statements public should not impose an unrealistic burden on relatively small entities with few stakeholders. No small enterprise—and possibly no SME—should be subject to compulsory financial statement audits. SMEs generally drive economic growth in LAC; heavy requirements for SMEs may serve as disincentives for businesses to operate in the formal sector.

Therefore, there is a need for a simplified accounting and financial reporting framework for SMEs, with requirements commensurate with their size, the types of transactions they conduct, and their limited range of stakeholders. A holistic approach would take into account SMEs' need for relief from excessive accounting and auditing (A&A) requirements, as well as their need for more time to implement appropriate standards effectively. Creating a simplified framework for SMEs would involve defining the attributes of company size; simplifying accounting standards; and reducing or eliminating various requirements for statutory audits, financial reporting, and dissemination of financial reports.

There is no internationally accepted definition for SMEs; LAC countries need to develop their own definitions, suited to their particular needs and business environment. Countries use different parameters and thresholds for defining SMEs: for example, the total amount of assets controlled, total revenues, total borrowings, and number of employees. The European Union characterizes as SMEs companies with two of the following three characteristics: (a) fewer than 250 employees, (b) annual revenues of less than €50 million (approximately US$70 million[2]), or (c) an annual balance sheet total not exceeding €43 million (US$60 million).

In Canada, SMEs are defined as having fewer than 500 employees and less than C\$50 million (US\$45 million) in annual revenues. It is considered good practice to use several parameters, not just one, to characterize SMEs. LAC countries should consider these types of parameters when drawing up their own, country-specific definitions of large, medium, small, and microenterprises.

Priority Reform: Provide Relief for SMEs

A simplified set of financial reporting standards would make it easier for SMEs to improve the quality of their financial information and, ultimately, to use that information to access credit. The International Accounting Standards Board (IASB) recently issued a simplified set of standards for financial reporting (referred to as "IFRS for SMEs" or "IFRS for Private Entities") that requires a lesser level of disclosure and eliminates the most complex options provided in IFRS, especially those requiring the use of fair values. The authorities in most LAC countries should consider adopting these standards for use by local SMEs—although there is legitimate concern in some countries that these standards might still be challenging to apply for entities at the smaller end of the corporate spectrum.

Other Important Reforms

Countries should also consider strengthening the financial reporting requirements applicable to SOEs, which have generally been left out of private sector reform efforts in LAC. Good international practice requires large SOEs to meet the same standards for accounting, auditing, reporting, and governance as listed companies (OECD 2005). This would entail, among other things, requiring the application of IFRS, annual independent audits, and the publication of financial statements.

Pillar 1	Priority reform
Setting adequate requirements	• Provide relief for small and medium enterprises through simplified requirements

Pillar 2: Developing Capacity in Accounting and Auditing

If corporate financial reporting standards are to be implemented properly, accounting professionals need to be adequately trained. Many LAC countries, particularly those that have adopted IFRS, have made efforts to train their accounting professionals and academics by offering training courses. Some of these efforts have been supported by the donor community, most notably the Inter-American Development Bank's (IDB's) Multilateral Investment Fund (MIF), which funded IFRS training in nine LAC countries. In addition, continuing professional development (CPD) is mandatory in seven LAC countries (table 3.4), and almost all professional bodies in the other countries offer CPD courses on a voluntary or compulsory basis.

Creating a certification system for the accounting profession is one way to help ensure that accountants have adequate capacity. While training is an important part of an overall capacity development process, it is not sufficient. It is difficult to assess not only the quality of the training that is offered, but also the extent to which the trainee retained the information. Creating a certification system, which culminates in a professional examination, is one way to ensure that new entrants into the profession have a minimum level of qualification. The creation of robust certification requirements can also bring other indirect benefits, including increased demand for high-quality accounting education at the university level, heightened prestige of the accounting profession, and enhanced oversight of supervised entities. In this regard, the International Federation of Accountants (IFAC) has issued International Education Standards for Professional Accountants (IES), which recommend the following as part of a certification process for the profession:

- A university education that meets minimum accounting curriculum requirements,
- At least three years' practice under an experienced mentor, and
- A qualifying examination.

External auditors, too, need to be subject to elevated entry requirements through a robust certification system. Most users of financial statements depend on the seal of quality that an external audit provides, so it is in the public interest that this cadre of professionals earn the credibility that results from consistently observing high auditing and ethics standards. Few LAC countries have established an effective certification system for auditors: the majority of auditors are not required to pass a professional examination to obtain a professional license, and most countries lack requirements for practical experience or CPD for practitioners. Moreover, even if minimum educational requirements are strengthened significantly, the improved training of professional accountants will rest on a system of accounting education that needs significant modernization in curriculum content and faculty capacity. Thus, the ability of preparers and auditors to comply with international standards (IFRS and ISA) is limited, and the quality of financial reporting in LAC reflects the unevenness of skills and training of the profession. Other regions are more advanced than LAC in regard to certification; box 7.1 briefly explains how certification systems work in four Asian countries.

Within LAC, Mexico's Contador Público Certificado credential stands out as a good practice that should be emulated. Mexico's creden-

---

Box 7.1

Cross-Regional Comparison: Certification Systems in Asia

To practice accountancy in most countries in East Asia and Pacific (EAP) and South Asia, an individual must usually pass an examination and complete practical training. In several countries, including in India, the number of candidates taking professional examinations has steadily increased over the years. In the Republic of Korea, the Ministry of Finance and Economy has a legal responsibility to conduct the professional accountant (CPA) examination, but has delegated the responsibility for administering the exam to the Financial Supervisory Service. In Sri Lanka, it is common practice to depend on the educational programs of the Institute of Chartered Accountants rather than universities for meeting educational requirements for entry into the accountancy profession. In the Philippines, eligibility to take the professional examination requires the applicant to be a citizen, hold a bachelor's degree in accountancy, and not have been convicted of any criminal offense. The table below shows the specific entry requirements, professional education, and training for these countries.

ROSC A&A reports in EAP and South Asia note the urgent need to enhance the resources available to teach A&A, both by updating the skills and knowledge of university staff and by providing the necessary textbooks and other training materials. University courses in accountancy do not always cover IFRS and ISA. In India, the curricula cover only Indian standards. In addition, both accounting course books and examinations lack adequate focus on the practical application

(Box continues on the following page.)

Box 7.1 (*continued*)

of standards. In the Philippines, the scarcity of locally developed instructional materials, student textbooks, and other learning materials is the main stumbling block in teaching up-to-date developments in accounting. In Sri Lanka, university education in accounting does not focus enough on the practical application of international standards.

Qualified professional accountants require further updating on recent developments in corporate financial reporting and related subjects. In this respect, many countries in EAP and South Asia have introduced a CPD requirement. ROSC A&A reports point out that monitoring and enforcement mechanisms for the CPD requirement still have not been put in place in many countries.

Entry and CPD Requirements in Four Asian Countries

	Passing the professional examination	Minimum practical training (in years)	Mandatory CPD
India	✓	3	✓
Philippines	✓	3	✓
Korea, Rep. of	✓	1	✓
Sri Lanka	✓	3	

Source: ROSC A&A reports.

tial is recognized in Canada and the United States, and has requirements that are in line with other internationally recognized certifications. To establish this credential, the Mexican accounting professional body (IMCP) successfully undertook a series of reforms to align its education and training requirements with those of the United States and Canada. The prestige of the Mexican profession has been elevated accordingly.

Priority Reform: Professional Accountant Certification

Pillar 2	Priority reform
Developing capacity in accounting and auditing	• Establish a certification system, focusing on external auditors

Instituting a certification process involves sweeping changes that affect a wide range of interested parties, particularly universities; therefore, stakeholder engagement is critical. In most LAC countries, universities have de facto power to license auditors and may be loath to give it up or share it. In addition, some auditors who entered the profession under old rules may not be receptive to a change that would affect their acquired rights. Therefore, when creating a certification system, it is important to engage stakeholders, particularly universities and the audit profession, from the beginning of the process. It helps to create grandfathering schemes so that auditors who are already practicing may continue to do so. In addition, the statutory framework must allow for certification. The case of Brazil illustrates what can happen when stakeholders are not sufficiently on board and the necessary statutory changes have not been made: a qualifying examination was instituted by the legally sanctioned accounting professional body (CFC), but a group of practitioners filed a lawsuit alleging that relevant Brazilian statutes required only a university degree to enter the profession and that the additional requirements introduced by CFC had no legal basis. The court ruled in favor of the plaintiffs, and the examination has been suspended.

Expanding requirements for auditor registration in regulated sectors may be one way to introduce a certification system. Financial sector and securities market regulators in many countries have created registries that auditors must join to audit regulated companies. One way to introduce a certification system incrementally would be to increase the requirements for inclusion on the auditor registry in line with IFAC's IES. For example, countries could begin to require an examination and professional experience as prequalifications to audit regulated companies. Over time, these requirements could be expanded to auditors of nonregulated companies. For this approach to work, however, it must be a joint effort involving regulators and the accounting professional bodies.

Other Important Reforms

As an added benefit, introducing a certification system would likely catalyze improvements in the tertiary education system. High-quality education at the tertiary level is essential to a robust accounting profession. While some attempts have been made to improve accounting curricula (see, for example, box 4.1), these efforts are not widespread. Issues relating to the quality of course content, the profile of professors, the quality and availability of teaching materials, research in accounting, and so on, all need to be addressed as part of any broad effort to reform A&A education. The introduction of a professional examination would also create demand for better accounting education at the tertiary level, as it would induce students to seek out schools capable of preparing them to pass the examination. In addition, to keep up with the constant evolution of new business practices, accountants need to update their knowledge and expand their skill sets continuously. LAC countries should strive to conform to IFAC's IES, which require at least 120 hours of CPD during each three-year period (an average of 40 hours per year).

Pillar 3: Enforcement

Ensuring PIEs' adherence to financial reporting obligations requires vigorous enforcement of accounting requirements (figure 7.3). While all PIEs have a certain degree of responsibility to the public, financial institutions (banks, insurance companies, savings and loan institutions, and so forth) should be subjected to stringent oversight, because they have fiduciary responsibilities to their depositors and policyholders and because instability in the financial sector would have a damaging ripple effect throughout the economy (as evi-

Figure 7.3 Enforcement

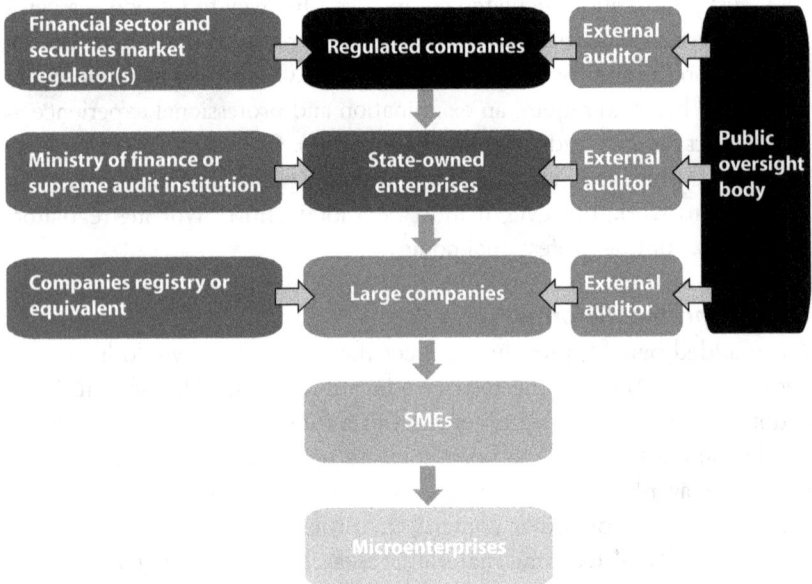

Source: Authors.

denced by the recent global economic crisis). Listed companies, too, have a very high degree of responsibility vis-à-vis their shareholders and investors and also require robust enforcement. Beyond this, some countries (for example, Argentina and Uruguay) have followed the European Union model, establishing a system of companies registries to which nonlisted companies are required to submit their financial statements for third parties to access.

There has been a trend toward stronger supervision of prudential requirements in the LAC region's financial sector. This was emphasized by the General Manager of the Bank for International Settlements, Jaime Caruana, who stated at a recent meeting of central banks and banking supervisors, "Domestic banks in Latin America have weathered [the current financial crisis] well thanks to the more effective regulation and oversight introduced in recent years" (Caruana 2009). While prudential supervision for financial institutions has been strengthened significantly in the region, more attention needs to be paid to general-purpose financial reporting (including the quality of disclosures and the treatment of off-balance-sheet entities) by listed companies and financial institutions. The ROSC A&A assessments have found that while securities market regulators have generally adequate statutory enforcement powers, they often lack the necessary complement of suitably qualified staff to carry out effective enforcement actions. Furthermore, most regulatory regimes in the region lack credible public sanctions.

On the audit side, adequate enforcement of professional standards is needed to safeguard public trust in the audit function. Independent audit oversight bodies that are responsible for monitoring and enforcing professional requirements now replace self-regulation arrangements in many countries, including the United States, European Union countries, and Japan. Most LAC countries have yet to put in place an effective system of independent oversight; they leave enforcement of auditing and ethical standards to the professional bodies themselves. However, the traditional self-regulation arrangements have proven to be unsatisfactory because they provide insufficient incentives to carry out in-depth inspections and to impose sanctions on members.

Pillar 3	Priority reforms
Enforcement	• Enforcement of regulated entities • Public oversight for the audit profession

Priority Reforms: Enforcement and Oversight

Enforcement of financial reporting requirements for regulated entities.
Robust enforcement requires adequate mechanisms to monitor compliance with financial reporting requirements, as well as a significant investment in recruiting and training an adequate number of qualified staff. In some countries, enforcement efforts often focus on form-related issues (for example, ensuring all financial reports are submitted on time, making basic calculations to ensure the numbers add up, enforcing deadlines). Although such efforts are a step in the right direction, enforcement tends to fall short when it comes to substance-related matters because strong monitoring mechanisms are not in place and enforcement staff often lack a comprehensive understanding of financial reporting issues. Regulators need to put in place thorough monitoring procedures, which should be clearly detailed in supervision manuals. In addition, enforcement staff must be well trained, so that they are able to analyze companies' financial statements and auditor reports systematically (using appropriate sampling techniques), identify instances of noncompliance, ask questions of the company or its auditors, require the necessary corrections or a restatement, and recommend appropriate resolution or sanctions.

In some countries, sanctions are too insignificant to deter noncompliance (for example, low fines). Appropriate sanctions that are disseminated transparently are needed to serve as a deterrent to noncompliance. In addition, publication of sanctions is useful, not only to promote compliance with rules, but to inform, and therefore protect, the public. Therefore, regulators should make sanctions public in a way that is easily accessible, as on their Web sites. It is important to ensure that all pertinent information on sanctions (for example, description of the violation and nature of sanction applied) can be easily found.

In countries where the financial sector is relatively small, it makes sense to consolidate enforcement efforts into one agency. Creating a robust enforcement regime requires significant resources—for example, for staff, information technology, and office space for a regulatory body. Smaller countries, in particular, would benefit from consolidating enforcement activities for regulated companies. This has been done in Colombia, where, since 2005, the Financial Superintendency is responsible for supervising banks, insurance companies, and listed companies.

Public oversight of the audit profession. Independent audit oversight bodies have replaced professional self-regulation in many countries, acting as regulators and supervisors for the audit profession. Much like other regulators, a public oversight body is responsible for enforcing professional standards through inspections of auditors and application of sanctions for noncompliance. It also maintains an auditor licensing and registration process, sets audit and ethical standards, and reports to the public—that is, taking over many of the functions that are currently in the domain of the accounting profession (via professional bodies). Audit oversight boards are most effective if they are independent of the audit profession—that is, the majority of board members should be nonpractitioner representatives of regulatory agencies and other concerned public institutions (for example, securities market supervisors, central bank, and ministry of finance), academia, the business community, and civil society groups. Various options are available for introducing a system of independent oversight; box 7.2 describes the structure and specific roles of audit oversight systems in Korea and Sri Lanka.

Establishing an independent audit oversight body is unquestionably difficult, involving significant resources. For the foreseeable future, establishing independent audit oversight systems in LAC—as in Japan and many European Union countries—will likely require financial support from the national government's budget. Because private- and financial-sector-led growth is central to the development of most LAC countries, and given the public-good nature of sound corporate financial reporting (with benefits ranging from creating a business climate conducive to economic development to promoting financial stability), governments have a vested interest in ensuring that auditors effectively discharge their function in accordance with applicable professional standards. (El Salvador provides an example of oversight systems funded by the government, and the challenges associated with them; see box 3.3.) Once the system has begun operating, it makes sense to require registered audit firms or sole practitioners to contribute to the oversight system through registration fees. However, in smaller countries, registration fees are unlikely to yield much, and continued government support will likely be necessary.

An oversight system is most effective in countries where the overall capacity of the audit profession is relatively strong. For such a system to work effectively, the oversight body needs to be staffed with individuals with a high degree of technical expertise, and the overall quality of audits in the country should be relatively satisfactory. In countries with low audit capacity, independent oversight should be approached as a long-term objective; it may help to focus first on activities to build capacity within

Box 7.2

Cross-Regional Comparison: Audit Oversight Systems in Korea and Sri Lanka

Several countries in the East Asia and Pacific (EAP) and South Asia regions have agreed to the need for effective systems of independent oversight of the audit profession to protect the public interest. In Korea, an ad hoc institution, the Financial Supervisory Service, is now responsible for audit oversight. In Sri Lanka, the Accounting and Auditing Standards Monitoring Board was established. The ROSC A&A reports for EAP and South Asia noted that public oversight bodies are in most cases constrained by the lack of adequate technical expertise and resources.

Characteristics	Korea	Sri Lanka
Name	Financial Supervisory Service (FSS)	The Sri Lanka Accounting and Auditing Standards Monitoring Board (SLAASMB)
Year established	1999 (established under the Act on the Establishment of Financial Supervisory Organization)	1995 (established under the Sri Lanka Accounting and Auditing Standards Act)
Structure	Headed by the Governor and organized along 25 departments and 16 offices	Governed by 13 members from academia, accountancy bodies, regulators, and commerce
Primary function and specific roles	Examination and supervision of financial institutions as well as other oversight and enforcement functions. Reviews the audit quality controls of major accounting firms, makes recommendations, and reports the results to the Securities and Futures Commission.	Monitoring and enforcement compliance with Sri Lanka accounting and auditing standards. The Board reviews selected financial statements and brings those cases requiring corrective measures to the attention of the particular enterprise. The Securities and Exchange Commission of Sri Lanka also agreed to refer cases of noncompliance.
Sanctions	Monetary fines and restrictions on securities issuance.	Monetary fines and penalties extending up to five years' imprisonment.
Web site	http://english.fss.or.kr/fsseng/index.jsp	www.slaasmb.org

Sources: ROSC A&A reports; FSS and SLAASMB Web sites.

the profession, such as creating certification systems and requiring CPD. For countries with more acute constraints on capacity or resources, the best option would probably be to build on the auditor oversight mechanisms already in place for regulated entities. In many LAC countries, regulators have already taken the lead in conducting inspections of auditors for companies under their purview; it may be worthwhile to build on such mechanisms, with a view to expanding the range of auditors being inspected over time. Countries that have not yet introduced that sort of system may find it a useful first step toward comprehensive oversight.

Other Important Reforms

Increased attention should be devoted to the enforcement of financial reporting requirements for other PIEs, particularly SOEs. In most LAC countries, the supreme audit institution (SAI)—which is mainly responsible for monitoring budget execution of government programs—is also responsible for oversight of SOEs, including acting as external auditor for them. However, because SAIs often lack the human and financial resources to conduct timely audits of SOEs, countries should consider establishing an ad hoc government body that is responsible for the financial oversight of SOEs. This body should also exercise the state's ownership function over such enterprises on behalf of citizens, safeguarding the equity value of the companies and limiting their contingent liabilities. The proposed body could be an entity within an existing institution, such as the ministry of finance, or it could be an independent agency created for this sole purpose. Chile, for example, has established an independent high commission that is responsible for supervising the performance of SOEs, including appointing members to their boards of directors. Regardless of whether the oversight body is a separate entity, it should be accountable to the national congress or parliament.

The Role of the World Bank and Other Development Partners

The donor community has a direct stake in corporate-sector A&A reforms, which affect countries' development agendas. First, sound corporate accounting, reporting, and auditing practices are necessary to achieve sustainable, private sector–led growth, which ranks high in many LAC countries' development strategies. Improved financial management and transparency in SOEs are critical for advancing the governance agenda, promoting macroeconomic stability, and improving the effectiveness of service delivery by these companies. Finally, strengthening the capacity of the accounting profession can help safeguard the efficient use of external assistance.

Several institutions have been providing technical assistance and capacity building. The multidonor Financial Sector Reform and Strengthening (FIRST) Initiative has funded technical assistance projects in Chile, El Salvador, Honduras, and Peru. With regard to capacity building, the IDB's MIF has provided grant funding in several countries for training-of-trainers programs in IFRS, among other initiatives.

In addition, the World Bank has engaged in both lending and nonlending activities to improve corporate financial reporting:

- *Development policy loans.* Since 2005, the World Bank has provided a number of development policy loans (DPLs) to member countries, to support reforms and capacity development efforts in areas that are key for economic development and poverty reduction. In LAC, recent DPLs support reforms in the field of corporate financial reporting: in Uruguay, the 2007 Institutional Building DPL includes a series of policy reforms aimed at supporting the adoption of IFRS and strengthening the independent oversight of the audit function; and in Paraguay's 2009 DPL, the focus has been on improving the financial oversight of SOEs.
- *Investment loans and credits.* In recent years, the World Bank has also provided technical assistance loans aimed at improving the corporate financial reporting framework, either as standalone operations or as part of a larger project. In the LAC region, the World Bank is financing a US$12.1 million Institutional Building Technical Assistance Loan to Uruguay. The loan includes a US$2.05 million component to support capital markets and corporate transparency reforms, with the aim of "strengthening corporate financial reporting framework in order to boost private investment, ensure financial sector stability and improve the governance of state-owned enterprises."
- *Knowledge-sharing initiatives and communities of practice.* The World Bank has also taken advantage of information and communications technology to promote dialogue and knowledge sharing. For example, it has used the Global Development Learning Network platform to organize a series of videoconference-based seminars in which leading specialists from around the world discuss A&A issues with participants from several LAC countries. Seminars have focused on such topics as IFRS for SMEs, insurance accounting, public oversight of the audit profession, and IFRS in the banking sector.[3]

- **CReCER Regional Conferences.**[4] The World Bank has also partnered with IFAC and the IDB to organize the CReCER conference on Accounting and Accountability for Regional Economic Growth, which has brought together several hundred participants from around the region and the world in Mexico (2007) and San Salvador (2008). This conference is paired with a public Web site, www.creceramericas.org, which serves as a knowledge repository for those who cannot attend the conference. The third CReCER conference is scheduled for September 2009 in São Paulo.

Now more than ever, the ROSC A&A is an important piece of the portfolio of analytic products that the World Bank offers to countries seeking to bring their practices up to par with international standards. The ROSC A&A program is one way the World Bank leverages global knowledge to support development at the country level. It is especially useful to middle-income countries, which are generally poised to adopt the reforms necessary to compete on a global playing field. It also contributes to international financial stability, which is important to all countries.

The global financial crisis, which continues to unfold in most of the world's largest economies, has reemphasized the importance of A&A. The focus on accounting issues during the November 2008 G-20 meeting of heads of states and governments in Washington was unprecedented for such a high-level meeting. To a significant degree, the crisis has pointed to a number of failures in the financial reporting process, and to the need for improvements in the design of international standards (especially fair value measurement and disclosure) and in their effective application at the country level.

Considering the serious damage to investor confidence caused by the crisis, a commonly shared expectation is that investors and lenders will place an even higher focus on high-quality financial reporting. For instance, the IASB has revised two of its standards on financial instruments (IAS 39 and IFRS 7); and in April 2009, the U.S. Financial Accounting Standards Board issued three "Final Staff Positions" to "improve guidance and disclosures on fair value measurements and impairments."

On the auditing side, even if the role played by external auditors has not been questioned in the same way as it was during the wave of corporate failures at the beginning of the decade, some significant reexamination is likely. The scandal surrounding India's Satyam Group at the beginning of 2009 has already triggered renewed debate about the benefits of a system of independent, public oversight of auditors. The issues of the governance of accounting professional bodies and the extent to which they advance the public interest will also be closely scrutinized. Now that IFAC has completed its "Clarity Project" to improve the quality of text in the ISAs, two specific issues will receive closer attention: (a) auditing fair value measurements and disclosures, and (b) the going concern issue (that is, whether a company whose financial statements are being audited retains the ability to function as a business entity in the foreseeable future).

The crisis will also likely result in renewed efforts to harmonize financial sector standards and to establish effective consolidated supervision. One of the key proposals arising from the April 2009 G-20 summit in London was to reestablish the Financial Stability Forum, which promotes international financial stability through information exchange and international cooperation in financial supervision and surveillance, as a Financial Stability Board with a broadened mandate and increased resources.

The emphasis on adopting strong international standards is not limited to developing countries; in fact, most of the reforms spawned by the current crisis are likely to begin in the United States and the European Union. At the G-20 summit in London, the final declaration emphasized the need for continued efforts to pursue and maintain financial stability, highlighting the importance of the 12 key international standards and codes on which ROSC reports are based. The assembled countries called for the World Bank and the International Monetary Fund to continue to carry out ROSC assessments and other measures to promote common implementation of international financial standards.

In the eight years since the ROSC A&A program was initiated, the world has made much progress toward common international standards of financial transparency, accountability, and governance. The LAC region has not been at the leading edge of this movement, but there have been bright spots and signs of growing momentum for reform. These trends are encouraging for everyone concerned with financial stability and the private sector–led development that strong A&A standards are meant to promote. The current financial crisis provides LAC countries the opportunity to narrow their financial reporting gap relative to other emerging regions. The authors of this book hope for continued and accelerated progress along this road in the coming years.

Notes

1. These factors draw upon the IASB's definition of public interest entities; see Box 2.1 for more information.
2. Converted using exchange rate on June 9, 2009.
3. See www.gdln.org for more information on the GDLN program.
4. CReCER is a Spanish-language acronym that stands for Contabilidad y Responsabilidad para el Crecimiento Económico Regional (Accounting and Accountability for Regional Economic Growth) and literally means "to grow."

About the ROSC Accounting and Auditing Program

A series of financial crises led to the World Bank's increased involvement in reporting on the observance of accounting and auditing (A&A) standards in partner countries. The Reports on the Observance of Standards and Codes (ROSC) initiative was established in 1999 in response to the international financial crises of the 1990s, which originated in Mexico, Asia, the Russian Federation, and Brazil. Before then, the international financial community—mainly the International Monetary Fund (IMF) and the World Bank—had taken a reactive role to financial crises by providing ex post support to stabilize the economies of the affected countries. However, the severity of these crises and their quick and widespread contagion throughout the developing world forced international financial institutions to rethink their strategy. They agreed that more needed to be done beforehand to strengthen the international financial architecture—particularly in emerging economies—and make it more resilient to shocks. Leaders at international financial institutions emphasized the need to create or observe internationally recognized standards and codes of good practice to strengthen the international financial architecture (Rubin 1998).

It was in this context that the World Bank and the IMF launched the ROSC program, focusing on 12 sets of internationally recognized core standards and codes,[1] including A&A. The World Bank and the IMF divided the responsibility for assessing the adherence to these sets of standards and codes, and the responsibility for the ROSC A&A module fell to the World Bank.

Goals of the ROSC A&A Program

The ROSC A&A evaluates a country's overall A&A framework, focusing not only on the standards themselves but also on their actual application and enforcement and on the overall enabling environment—ranging from the enforcement regimes to the professional qualifications of accountants and auditors—that underpins A&A practices in partner countries. Specifically, the ROSC A&A assesses the following:

- The strengths and weaknesses of existing institutional frameworks (for example, A&A rules and requirements, effectiveness of monitoring and enforcement mechanisms)
- The enabling environment for A&A (for example, organization of the accounting profession and capacity of its members, quality of accounting education)
- The comparability of national A&A standards with International Financial Reporting Standards (IFRS) and International Standards on Auditing (ISA), respectively
- The degree to which corporate entities comply with established A&A standards in the country.

The main focus of the ROSC A&A is on the quality of financial reporting by public interest entities in the private sector—for example, listed companies and financial institutions. It also covers state-owned enterprises, depending on their importance in the economic context of the country, and small and medium enterprises.

Coverage of the ROSC A&A Program

In the 10 years since the ROSC A&A was created, more than 75 country reports have been completed, 17 of them for the Latin America and Caribbean (LAC) region. Completed reports, cleared by the respective governments, are posted on the World Bank's Web site. The table below summarizes the state of the ROSC A&A program in LAC (see also appendix B). A broad discussion of the ROSC A&A program, its intellectual underpinnings, and its early results is provided on the ROSC Web site (http://www.worldbank.org/ifa/rosc_aa.html).

ROSC A&A Reports in the LAC Region – Status in June 2009

Published	Date of review	In draft or pending publication	In pipeline
Argentina	July 2007	Guatemala	Costa Rica
Brazil	June 2005	Panama	Guyana
Chile	June 2004	Dominican Republic Update	Nicaragua
Colombia	July 2003		
Dominican Republic	December 2004		
Eastern Caribbean States	June 2008		
Ecuador	March 2004		
El Salvador	June 2005		
Haiti	November 2007		
Honduras	May 2007		
Jamaica	June 2003		
Mexico	March 2004		
Paraguay	June 2006		
Peru	June 2004		
Uruguay	January 2006		

Note

1. The 12 standards are data dissemination, fiscal transparency, transparency in monetary and financial policies, banking supervision, securities market regulation, insurance supervision, payments and settlements, anti-money laundering, corporate governance, accounting, auditing, and insolvency and creditor rights.

Coverage of ROSC A&A Program in Latin America and the Caribbean

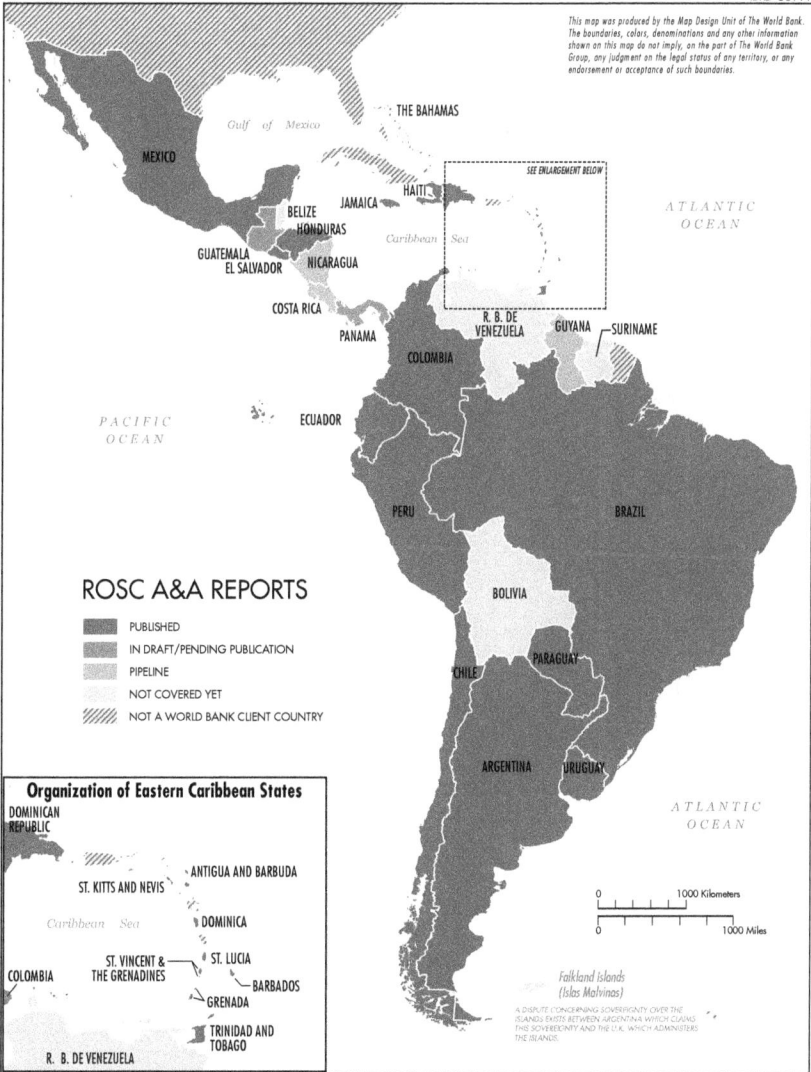

IBRD 36999

This map was produced by the Map Design Unit of The World Bank. The boundaries, colors, denominations and any other information shown on this map do not imply, on the part of The World Bank Group, any judgment on the legal status of any territory, or any endorsement or acceptance of such boundaries.

THE BAHAMAS

Gulf of Mexico

MEXICO

HAITI
JAMAICA
BELIZE
HONDURAS
GUATEMALA
EL SALVADOR   NICARAGUA

SEE ENLARGEMENT BELOW

ATLANTIC
OCEAN

Caribbean   Sea

COSTA RICA

PANAMA

R. B. DE
VENEZUELA   GUYANA   SURINAME

COLOMBIA

PACIFIC
OCEAN

ECUADOR

PERU

BRAZIL

ROSC A&A REPORTS

BOLIVIA

- PUBLISHED
- IN DRAFT/PENDING PUBLICATION
- PIPELINE
- NOT COVERED YET
- NOT A WORLD BANK CLIENT COUNTRY

PARAGUAY

CHILE

ARGENTINA   URUGUAY

Organization of Eastern Caribbean States

DOMINICAN
REPUBLIC

ANTIGUA AND BARBUDA
ST. KITTS AND NEVIS

Caribbean   Sea

DOMINICA

COLOMBIA

ST. VINCENT &
THE GRENADINES

ST. LUCIA

BARBADOS

GRENADA

TRINIDAD AND
TOBAGO

R. B. DE VENEZUELA

ATLANTIC
OCEAN

0   1000 Kilometers

0   1000 Miles

Falkland Islands
(Islas Malvinas)

A DISPUTE CONCERNING SOVEREIGNTY OVER THE
ISLANDS EXISTS BETWEEN ARGENTINA WHICH CLAIMS
THE SOVEREIGNTY AND THE U.K. WHICH ADMINISTERS
THE ISLANDS.

JULY 2009

IFRS Adoption in Latin America and the Caribbean

STATUS OF IFRS ADOPTION

IBRD 36986

This map was produced by the Map Design Unit of The World Bank. The boundaries, colors, denominations and any other information shown on this map do not imply, on the part of The World Bank Group, any judgment on the legal status of any territory, or any endorsement or acceptance of such boundaries.

JULY 2009

Country Action Plans: Developing a Strategic Vision for Reform and an Agenda for Action

Countries participating in the Reports on the Observance of Standards and Codes, Accounting and Auditing (ROSC A&A) program have begun drawing up comprehensive Country Action Plans (CAPs) to implement the ROSC policy recommendations. While the ROSC teams strive to make the ROSC recommendations as specific as possible, and to sequence them as short-, medium-, and long-term reforms, they provide only general policies that must then be transformed into a prioritized set of activities. For example, while the ROSC may recommend developing a set of standards for small and medium enterprises (SMEs), a CAP sets out all the specific actions to achieve this objective—for example, round-table discussions with SME groups and other stakeholders, analysis of SME standards in other countries, review of the existing legal framework to map out what needs to be changed—providing deadlines for each action and identifying the parties responsible for each action.

Like the ROSC A&A report, the CAP should take a holistic view of the country's reform requirements in the context of the broader strategy for private and financial sector development. In this regard, one of the first steps consists of forming a multidisciplinary group with the responsibility of developing the CAP and implementing it. This group, often referred to as the National Steering Committee (NSC), is usually headed by a high authority in government, such as the ministry of finance, and includes all the parties that would be responsible for carrying out the activities in the CAP. The NSC is responsible for determining the reforms to be included in the CAP, their order of priority, and the time frame for each activity. While there are no hard rules for preparing a CAP, this appendix provides a number of guidelines for preparing a high-quality plan.

1. Reforms focus on simple and enforceable measures.

Activities involving highly demanding and sophisticated regulations are not necessarily good practice. Before instituting a new requirement, the NSC should consider the capacity of both the private sector and the profession to comply with proposed requirements, and of the regulators to enforce them. A rule that looks good on paper but cannot be enforced is often worse than no rule at all. Consistent nonenforcement nurtures a culture of noncompliance, which, once entrenched, becomes difficult to reverse. In this regard, the NSC should analyze the costs and benefits associated with each new regulation, including the costs companies must bear to comply with the regulation and the enforcement costs to the government (for example, the costs of creating and staffing an enforcement body, and of sustaining that body in the medium and long term).

Taking incremental steps can help. Activities can start small, and then be scaled up over time, as capacity and resource levels allow. For instance, in Uruguay, a project to improve "informational transparency" in the private sector, launched in 2007 with support from the World Bank, initially focused on a seemingly easy step: reaching an agreement between the Uruguayan authorities and the International Accounting Standards Committee Foundation (which owns the copyright on the International Financial Reporting Standards, or IFRS) for the use and dissemination of IFRS. Since then, the authorities have been working on strengthening the national accounting standard setter, the Permanent Commission on Accounting Standards. Eventually the government introduced, and the Congress passed, a bill to adopt the full, up-to-date version of IFRS in the country.

2. Sequencing: Reforms are prioritized.

A number of considerations come into play when deciding which reforms need to be carried out first, and which can wait. There is no standardized way to determine which reforms should take priority; it depends on country circumstances. The NSC must consider factors such as the following:

- *Importance of the reform for the country's development agenda.* Some reforms are of particular importance for furthering the country's development agenda—for example, simplifying rules for SMEs to promote private sector development, strengthening rules for banks to ensure financial sector stability—and should be given greater weight and priority.
- *Availability of resources.* The NSC must take into consideration the human and financial resources available for carrying out the reform, and the sustainability of the reform; thus, it is desirable to consider cost-recovering activities.
- *Human capacity.* The NSC must determine if the reform can be undertaken with existing capacity in the public and private sectors, or if capacity building is a prerequisite.
- *Political environment.* If the political environment is favorable or there is a strong champion in government, it may be worthwhile to pursue a reform even if it is not particularly pressing, as it may become very difficult to carry out once the political winds change.
- *External factors.* Some reforms must be carried out as a precondition to some important national objective (for example, entering into a trade agreement or obtaining international financing).

Sometimes it may be worthwhile to take on relatively unimportant reforms early on, especially if they provide the foundation for other key reforms or if they are "low-hanging fruit"—that is, reforms that can be achieved relatively easily and quickly, with little if any opposition. Uruguay's passage of a law updating the version of IFRS that is legally mandated is a recent example of such relatively easy measures. It is often advantageous to begin a reform program with such straightforward gains, which achieve quick wins and generate momentum for the broader reform process.

3. All key stakeholders play an active role.

A wide range of groups have a stake in corporate sector A&A reform initiatives, and their participation in the CAP process is essential. Companies are required to comply with accounting standards in preparing their financial statements; auditors apply auditing standards; investors and lenders want the financial information presented to them to be reliable; regulators (for example, banking, insurance, and securities market supervisors, as well as tax authorities) are responsible for ensuring that accounting, auditing, and reporting requirements are being met; policy makers, including legislators, are expected to enact relevant statutory requirements; and academics play a critical role in preparing the next generation of accounting and business professionals. A successful CAP involves all relevant stakeholders from the outset, seeking their views and buy-in. Although it may seem at first that involving such a large and diverse group would prolong the process, in fact it has the opposite effect. While the early discussions may be lengthier, there will be less resistance to the CAP once it is complete, and its activities will be implemented more smoothly and quickly.

4. The government plays a leading role as coordinator and facilitator.

The government has an important role to play in leading the reform process overall. In most countries, only a high government official has the convening power to bring together all the various stakeholder groups and compel them to work together as part of the NSC. In addition, since only the government has the authority to issue statutory rules, which are required as part of many of the reforms under a CAP, it is important that the government lead the CAP process. However, the government should not crowd out other stakeholders. Before assigning a reform activity to the public sector, the NSC must consider whether government actions will encourage or discourage actions by other stakeholders.

5. Cooperating with other countries is also part of the solution.

Many of the reforms in corporate A&A would benefit from cooperation between countries at a regional or subregional level. Reforms that involve significant policy shifts might be complicated for a country—particularly a small one—to take on by itself. Some have advocated, for instance, creating a common oversight system for auditors on a subregional level (for example, for Central American countries), considering the significant economies of scale this would enable. Even when joint solutions are not feasible, countries would benefit from exchanging experiences and knowing some of the lessons learned by their neighbors or countries that have common characteristics and face similar issues.

An instructive example of international cooperation is the consultations that took place among Canada, Mexico, and the United States to achieve mutual recognition of accounting professional licenses in those three countries. This understanding enables an accountant licensed in Mexico to practice in the United States and Canada without having to take the complete professional entry-level examinations of these two countries. Instead, Mexican certified accountants (CPC) are simply required to pass a test on taxation and other legal differences between Mexico and the United States.

References and Other Resources

Reports on the Observance of Standards and Codes, Accounting and Auditing

The ROSC A&A reports on which this book draws follow, and are available at http://www.worldbank.org/ifa/rosc_aa.html.

Argentina (2007). Henri Fortin, Ana Cristina Hirata Barros.

Brazil (2005). Henri Fortin, Ana Cristina Hirata Barros.

Chile (2004). Henri Fortin and Craig Walter.

Colombia (2003). M. Zubaidur Rahman and Luis Schwarz.

Dominican Republic (2004). Henri Fortin, Luis Gómez Nina, Andrés Terrero.

Dominican Republic Update (2009). Henri Fortin, David Martínez Muñoz, and Michelle Tejada.

Eastern Caribbean States (2008). Kit Cutler, Henri Fortin, and Svetlana Klimenko.

Ecuador (2004). Henri Fortin.

El Salvador (2005). Henri Fortin.

Guatemala (2009). Henri Fortin.

Haiti (2007). Henri Fortin and Fily Sissoko.

Honduras (2007). Henri Fortin and Ana Cristina Hirata Barros.

Jamaica (2003). David Cairns and M. Zubaidur Rahman.

Mexico (2004). Henri Fortin, M. Zubaidur Rahman, and Luis Schwarz.

Panama (2009). Kit Cutler and Henri Fortin.

Paraguay (2006). Orlando Ferreira and Henri Fortin.

Peru (2004). Henri Fortin and Alfredo Rodríguez Neira.

Uruguay (2006). Orlando Ferreira, Henri Fortin, and Joanne Givens.

References

American Institute of Chartered Public Accountants. 2008. "Code of Professional Conduct." AICPA, New York.

Andrade, Luis, Diana Farrell, and Susan Lund. 2007. "Fulfilling the Potential of Latin America's Financial Systems." *The McKinsey Quarterly*, May.

Barayre-El Shami, Cécile. 2008. "Building a Legal Framework for the Information Economy." Presentation to UNCTAD Joint Facilitation Meeting on E-Commerce as a Key Facilitator for SME Competitiveness, May 22, in Geneva, Switzerland.

Basel Committee on Banking Supervision. 2002. "The Relationship between Banking Supervisors and Banks' External Auditors." Bank for International Settlements, Basel, Switzerland.

————. 2008. *External Audit Quality and Banking Supervision*. Basel, Switzerland: Bank for International Settlements.

Bernanke, Ben S. 2005. "Inflation in Latin America: A New Era?" Speech at the Stanford Institute for Economic Policy Research Economic Summit, February 11, in Stanford, California.

Borgonovo, Alfred. 2009. "Accounting Education in Panama." Report on a Project to Improve Accounting Education in Central America. Unpublished, World Bank, Washington, DC.

Brackney, Kennard S., and Philip R. Witmer. 2005. "The European Union's Role in International Standards Setting: Will Bumps in the Road to Convergence Affect the SEC's Plans?" *The CPA Journal* 25 (11).

Bradshaw, Mark T., Brian J. Bushee, and Gregory S. Miller. 2004. "Accounting Choice, Home Bias, and U.S. Investment in Non-U.S. Firms." *Journal of Accounting Research* 42 (5): 795–841.

British Broadcasting Corporation. 2008. "Summary of the Impact that Adopting International Financial Reporting Standards Would Have on the BBC's Group Financial Statements 2007/2008." BBC, London.

Caruana, Jaime. 2009. "Financial Globalisation, the Crisis and Latin America." Speech delivered to the XLVI Meeting of Central Bank Governors of the American Continent and LXXXVII Meeting of Central Bank Governors of Latin America and Spain, May 14, in Santo Domingo, Dominican Republic.

Casey, William M., and Pietro Masci. 2003. "Valuation and Mergers and Acquisition in Latin America: Accounting Rules and the Functioning of Capital Markets." In *Handbook of World Stock, Derivative and Commodity Exchanges*. London: Mondo Visione.

Cheu, Ter Kim. 2007. "From 'Fussy' to 'Fuzzy': The Principles-Based Approach to Legislative Drafting." Presented at the Second Annual Event of the Attorney General's Chambers of Brunei Darussalam, Malaysia, and Singapore, April 19, Sabah, Malaysia.

Chiraz, Ben Ali, Samir Trabelsi, and Mireille Gettler Summa. 2007. "Disclosure Quality and Ownership Structure: Evidence from the French Stock Market." Paper presented at the Workshop on Accounting in Europe conference, September 12–13, Paris.

Ciesielski, Jack T. 2007. "It's Not A Small World, After All: The SEC Goes International." *Analyst's Accounting Observer* 16 (11).

Cihák, Martin, and Richard Podpiera. 2006. "Is One Watchdog Better Than Three? International Experience with Integrated Financial Sector Supervision." IMF Working Paper No. 06/57, International Monetary Fund, Washington, DC.

Collis, Jill. 2003. "Directors' Views on Exemption from the Statutory Audit: A Research Report for the DTI." UK Department for Business, Enterprise & Regulatory Reform, London.

Commission of the European Communities. 2008. "Report from the Commission to the Council and the European Parliament on the Operation of Regulation (EC) No 1606/2002 of 19 July 2002 on the Application of International Accounting Standards." Commission of the European Communities, Brussels.

Covrig, Vicentiu M., Mark L. Defond, and Mingyi Hung. 2007. "Home Bias, Foreign Mutual Fund Holdings, and the Voluntary Adoption of International Accounting Standards." *Journal of Accounting Research* 45 (1): 41–70.

de la Torre, Augusto, and Sergio L. Schmukler. 2007. *Emerging Capital Markets and Globalization: The Latin American Experience*. Washington, DC: World Bank.

de la Torre, Augusto, Juan Carlos Gozzi, and Sergio L. Schmukler. 2007a. "Capital Market Development: Whither Latin America?" Policy Research Working Paper No. 4156, World Bank, Washington, DC.

———. 2007b. "Financial Development: Maturing and Emerging Policy Issues." *World Bank Research Observer* 22 (1): 67–102.

Devlin, David. 2006. "Public Oversight of the Audit Profession." In "Advanced Program in Accounting and Auditing Regulation." World Bank, Washington, DC.

Devlin, Robert, and Ricardo Ffrench-Davis. 1995. "The Great Latin America Debt Crisis: A Decade of Asymmetric Adjustment." *Revista de Economia Política* 15 (3).

Diao, Xinshen, Eugenio Díaz-Bonilla, and Sherman Robinson. 2003. "Scenarios for Trade Integration in the Americas." *Economie internationale* 94–95: 33–51.

Dickerson, Reed. 1954. *Legislative Drafting*. Westport, CT: Greenwood Press.

Didriksson, Axel. 2008. "Global and Regional Contexts of Higher Education in Latin America and the Caribbean." In *Trends in Higher Education in Latin America and the Caribbean*, ed. Ana Lúcia Gazzola and Axel Didriksson. Cartagena: International Institute of UNESCO for Higher Education in Latin America and the Caribbean (IESALC-UNESCO).

Dye, Kenneth M., and Rick Stapenhurst. 1998. "Pillars of Integrity: The Importance of Supreme Audit Institutions in Curbing Corruption." Economic Development Institute of the World Bank, Washington, DC.

Economist. 2009. "Easier for a Camel: A Special Report on the Rich." *The Economist*, April 2.

Ernst & Young. 2008. "Global IPO Trends Report 2008." EYGM Limited, London.

European Commission Directorate General Internal Market and Services. 1999. "The Review of the Overall Financial Position of an Insurance Undertaking (Solvency II Review)." Document No. 2095/99, European Commission, Brussels.

Eurostat. 2009. "Euro Indicators." Press Release, May 15. Eurostat Press Office, Brussels.

Fan, Qimiao, Alberto Criscuolo, and Iva Ilieva-Hamel. 2005. "Whither SMEs?" Development Outreach Special Report: *A Better Investment Climate for Everyone*. Washington, DC: World Bank Institute.

FELABAN, FOMIN, and D'Alessio Irol. 2004. "Estudio sobre la Predisposición de las Entidades Financieras de Latinoamérica y Caribe para la Financiación de las Peque—as y Medianas Empresas." Bogotá: FELABAN. Cited in Rojas-Suarez, Liliana. 2007. "The Provision of Banking Services in Latin America: Obstacles and Recommendations." Working Paper No. 124, Center for Global Development, Washington, DC.

Fernández Lamarra, Norberto. 2006. "Los Sistemas de Evaluación y Acreditación de la Calidad de la Educación Superior en América Latina: Situación, problemas y perspectivas." In Dilvo Ristoff and Palmira Sevegnani (Eds.), *Modelos Institucionais de Educação Superior*, 19–66. Brasília, Brazil: Instituto Nacional de Estudos e Pesquisas Educacionais Anísio Teixeira.

Financial Accounting Standards Board (US). 2007. "Accounting Research Bulletin No. 51 (as amended by Financial Accounting Standard No. 160)." FASB, Norwalk, CT.

Fischer, Michael J. 2000. "Luca Pacioli on Business Profits." *Journal of Business Ethics* 25 (4): 299–312.

Friedman, Felice B., and Claire Grose. 2006. "Promoting Access to Primary Equity Markets: A Legal and Regulatory Approach." Policy Research Working Paper No. 3892, World Bank, Washington, DC.

Gacel-Ávila, Jocelyne, Isabel Cristina Jaramillo, Jane Knight, and Hans de Wit. 2005. "The Latin American Way: Trends, Issues, and Directions." In *Higher Education in Latin America: The International Dimension*, ed. Hans de Wit, Isabel Christina Jaramillo, Jocelyne Gacel-Ávila, and Jane Knight, 341–67. Washington, DC: World Bank.

Galeazzi Mora, Wladimiro. 1959. "Principios de Contabilidad Generalmente Aceptados." Speech delivered on June 19 in the Federal District, Mexico. http://www.cinif.org.mx/publicaciones_12.

García Herrero, Alicia, Javier Santillán Sonsoles Gallego, Lucía Cuadro, and Carlos Egea. 2002. "Latin American Financial Development in Perspective." Presented at the Seminar of the Eurosystem and Latin American Central Banks, May 23, in Madrid, Spain.

Geithner, Timothy, and Lawrence Summers. 2009. "A New Financial Foundation." *Washington Post*, June 15, Op-Ed section.

Gielen, Frédéric, Eric van der Plaats, Ana Cristina Hirata Barros, and Jennie Tranter. 2007. "Corporate Sector Accounting and Auditing Within the Acquis Communautaire—A Building Block of the Internal Market." World Bank, Washington, DC.

Government of Honduras. 2006. *Ley de transparencia y acceso a la información pública*. Decree No. 170-2006. Published in Official Gazette of Honduras dated December 30. Tegucigalpa.

Group of 20. 2009. "Declaration on Strengthening the Financial System." Communiqué from the G-20 Leaders Summit, April 2, in London, UK. http://www.g20.org.

Grumet, Lou. 2005. "Rethinking the 'Peer' in Peer Review." *Accounting Today*, September 26. http://www.webcpa.com.

Harrington, Cynthia. 2005. "The Accounting Profession: Looking Ahead." *The Journal of Accountancy* October.

Hayes, Margaret Daly. 1989. "The U.S. and Latin America: A Lost Decade?" *Foreign Affairs* 68 (1).

Hegarty, John, Frédéric Gielen, and Ana Cristina Hirata Barros. 2004. "Implementation of International Accounting and Auditing Standards: Lessons Learned from the World Bank's Accounting and Auditing ROSC Program." World Bank, Washington, DC.

Herz, Robert H. 2002. "Meeting the Challenges of Financial Reporting in an Era of Change." Speech delivered to the Financial Executives International Conference, November 4, in New York.

Holm-Nielsen, Lauritz B., Kristian Thorn, José Joaquín Brunner, and Jorge Balán. 2005. "Regional and International Challenges to Higher Education in Latin América." In *Higher Education in Latin America: The International Dimension*, ed. Hans de Wit, Isabel Christina Jaramillo, Jocelyne Gacel-Ávila, and Jane Knight, 39–70. Washington, DC: World Bank.

Hope, Ole-Kristian, Justin Jin, and Tony Kang. 2006. "Empirical Evidence on Jurisdictions that Adopt IFRS." *Journal of International Accounting Research* 5 (2): 39–68.

IASB (International Accounting Standards Board). 2004. *Preliminary Views on Accounting Standards for Small and Medium-sized Entities*. Discussion Paper Series. London: IASB.

———. 2006. "A Roadmap for Convergence between IFRSs and US GAAP—2006–2008: Memorandum of Understanding between the FASB and the IASB." IASB, London.

IFAC (International Federation of Accountants). 2005. *Code of Ethics for Professional Accountants*. New York: IFAC.

———. 2006. *Statements of Membership Obligations 1-7*. New York: IFAC.

———. 2008. *International Education Standards* 1–8. New York: IFAC.

———. 2009a. "Guidance on the Formation and Organization of a Professional Accountancy Body." CD-ROM toolkit. IFAC, New York.

———. 2009b. "IFAC Criteria and Process for Membership." IFAC, New York. http://www.ifac.org/About/Membership.php

International Monetary Fund. 2009. *Regional Economic Outlook: Western Hemisphere*. Washington, DC: IMF.

Laeven, Luc, and Fabian Valencia. 2008. "Systemic Banking Crises: A New Database." Working Paper No. 08/224, International Monetary Fund, Washington, DC.

LAN Airlines. 2008. "LAN Airlines S.A. Announces Accounting Policies and Expected Impact Related to the Adoption of IFRS." Press release, September 30, Santiago, Chile.

Loayza, Norman, Pablo Fajnzylber, and César Calderón. 2004. "Economic Growth in Latin America and the Caribbean: Stylized Facts, Explanations, and Forecasts." Working Paper Series 265, Central Bank of Chile, Santiago.

Loayza, Norman, and Luisa Palacios. 1997. "Economic Reform and Progress in Latin America and the Caribbean." Policy Research Working Paper No. 1829, World Bank, Washington, DC.

Madziar, Piotr. 2007. "The European Commission and the International Accounting Standards." Presentation to the SAGE European Accountants Conference, September 13–14, in Paris, France.

Márquez, Manuel, Alberto Barreix, and Luiz Villela. 2007. "Recommendations and Best Practices on Taxation of SMEs in Latin America." Paper presented at the International Tax Dialogue Global Conference on Taxation of Small and Medium Enterprises, October 17–19, in Buenos Aires, Argentina.

Meiers, Donald H. 2006. "The MD&A Challenge: The Difficulty of Crafting a Quality Disclosure." *Journal of Accountancy* 201 (1): 59–66.

Mexican National Banking and Securities Commission. 2008. Untitled press release No. 56. November 11. http://www.cnbv.gob.mx/recursos/056_Adopcion_IFRS_english.pdf.

OECD (Organisation for Economic Co-operation and Development). 2003. *Corporate Governance in Latin America*. Paris: OECD.

———. 2005. "Guidelines on Corporate Governance of State-Owned Enterprises." OECD, Paris.

———. 2006. "The SME Financing Gap (Vol. I): Theory and Evidence." OECD, Paris.

———. 2008. *Using the OECD Principles of Corporate Governance: A Boardroom Perspective*. Paris: OECD.

Ottaway, Marina. 2001. "Corporatism Goes Global: International Organizations, NGO Networks and Transnational Business." *Global Governance* 7 (3).

Pacioli, Luca. 1494. *Somma de Aritmetica, Geometria, Proporzion e Proporzionalità*. Venice.

Peek, Lucia, Maria Roxas, George Peek, Egbert McGraw, Yves Robichaud, and Jorge Castillo Villarreal. 2007. "NAFTA Professional Mutual Recognition Agreements: Comparative Analysis of Accountancy Certification and Licensure." *Global Perspectives on Accounting Education* 4 (1): 1–24.

Podpiera, Richard, and Martin Cihák. 2007. "Are More Integrated Prudential Supervision Agencies Characterized by Better Regulation and Supervision?" Paper presented at 2nd Annual Conference on Empirical Legal Studies, July 5, New York, New York.

Riding, Allan. 2006. *Working Capital Financing and the Canada Small Business Financing (CSBF) Program*. Ottawa: Small Business Policy Branch, Industry Canada.

Ragir, Alexander. 2007. "Tough Rules Draw Funds to Brazil." *International Herald Tribune*, March 8.

Rogoff, Kenneth. 2009. "Brave New Financial World." *The Korea Times*, March 29, Opinion section.

Rojas-Suarez, Liliana. 2007. "The Provision of Banking Services in Latin America: Obstacles and Recommendations." Working Paper No. 124, Center for Global Development, Washington, DC.

Rubin, Robert E. 1998. "Strengthening the Architecture of the International Financial System." Speech delivered at the Brookings Institution, April 14, in Washington, DC, USA.

Santana, Maria Helena, Melsa Ararat, Petra Alexandru, B. Burcin Yurtoglu, and Mauro Rodrigues da Cunha. 2008. "Novo Mercado and Its Followers: Case Studies in Corporate Governance Reform." Global Corporate Governance Forum, Washington, DC.

Schilder, Arnold. 2006. "Adoption of IFRS in the Banking Sector (Part I)." In Advanced Program in Accounting and Auditing Regulation" Module 23. World Bank, Washington, DC.

Seibert, Larry J. 2008. "What Members Value in Their Decision to Join or Renew Their Association Membership." White Paper, Center for Association Leadership, Washington, DC.

Street, Donna L. 2003. "GAAP Convergence 2002: A Survey of National Efforts to Promote and Achieve Convergence with International Financial Reporting Standards." Published jointly by the six largest international public accounting firms.

Sueyoshi, Ana. 2009. "Long-Term Economic Growth, Investment and Savings in Latin America and the Caribbean: Stylized Facts Since the 1960s." International Studies Department Research Paper No. 27, Utsunomiya University, Japan.

Thomadakis, Stavros B. 2005. "The Regulation of Audit: National Responses and the International Public Interest." Remarks delivered to the New Zealand Institute of Chartered Accountants, November 17, in Auckland, New Zealand.

Thornton, G. C. 1970. *Legislative Drafting*. London: Butterworths.

Tweedie, David. 2004. "International Accounting Standards Committee Foundation Annual Report 2004." International Accounting Standards Committee Foundation, London.

UK Department of Trade and Industry. 2003. "Review of the Regulatory Regime of the Accountancy Profession: Legislative Proposals." Document No. 03/589, UK Department of Trade and Industry, London.

UNCTAD-ISAR (United Nations Conference on Trade and Development, Intergovernmental Working Group of Experts on International Standards of Accounting and Reporting). 2003. *Revised Model Accounting Curriculum*. Geneva: UNCTAD.

U.S. Congress. 2002. *Sarbanes-Oxley Act of 2002*. Public Law 107-204. Enacted July 30, 2002.

U.S. SEC (United States Securities and Exchange Commission). 2007. "Acceptance From Foreign Private Issuers of Financial Statements Prepared in Accordance With International Financial Reporting Standards Without

Reconciliation to U.S. GAAP." Securities Act Release No. 33-8879; *Exchange Act Release* No. 34-57026.

———. 2008. "Roadmap for the Potential Use of Financial Statements Prepared in Accordance with International Financial Reporting Standards by US Issuers." Securities Act Release No. 33-8982, SEC, Washington, DC.

Wolk, Harry I., James L. Dodd, and John J. Rozycki. 2007 *Accounting Theory: Conceptual Issues in a Political and Economic Environment*, 7th Ed. Los Angeles: SAGE Publishers.

World Bank. 2002. *Constructing Knowledge Societies: New Challenges for Tertiary Education*. Washington, DC: World Bank.

———. 2005. "El Salvador Investment Climate Assessment" Vol. I. Report No. 32711-SV, World Bank, Washington, DC.

———. 2007. *World Development Indicators 2007*. Washington, DC: World Bank. http://www.worldbank.org.

———. 2008. *Migration and Remittances Factbook 2008*. Washington, DC: World Bank.

———. 2009a. *Global Development Finance 2009: Charting a Global Recovery*. Washington, DC: World Bank.

———. 2009b. "The Global Financial and Economic Storm: How Bad Is the Weather in Latin America and the Caribbean?" Briefing note prepared by the LAC Chief Economist's Office for the 2009 Spring Meetings, April 24, in Washington, DC.

Zoellick, Robert. 2007. "An Inclusive and Sustainable Globalization." Speech delivered at the National Press Club, October 10, Washington, DC.

Glossary

Accounting The system of recording and summarizing business and financial transactions and analyzing, verifying, and reporting the results.

Audit committee A committee, including at least one financial expert, reporting to the board of directors, formed for the purpose of overseeing a company's financial reporting and auditing. Audit committee members should be free from conflicts of interest and should not receive any compensation for their service on the committee. The audit committee selects and oversees the auditing firm and reviews the results of the audits.

Balance sheet A snapshot of a business's financial condition at a specific moment in time. A balance sheet comprises assets, liabilities, and owners' or stockholders' equity. It is an integral part of a set of complete financial statements.

Bookkeeping Systematic recording of a company's day-to-day financial transactions.

Cash-flow statement or statement of cash flows A statement that analyzes changes in cash and cash equivalents during a period. It is an integral part of a set of complete financial statements.

Certified or chartered public accountant Professional member of an accounting association that qualifies and licenses its members to provide accounting or auditing services. In many countries, a "certified" or "chartered" designation is required for professionals to conduct external audits.

Companies registrar or registrar of companies Government or quasi-governmental authority responsible for recording and maintaining certain details of new and existing firms within a jurisdiction (for example, company bylaws, names of shareholders, financial statements).

Continuing professional development (CPD) The means by which members of professional bodies maintain, improve, and broaden their knowledge and expertise as well as develop the required qualities in their profession. Accounting professional bodies may require their members to log a certain number of hours of CPD per year to maintain a license to practice. CPD may be achieved through training courses, postgraduate education, conference participation, or other means approved by the professional body.

Explanatory notes Notes that illustrate and analyze the financial statement data and contain all the information deemed necessary for providing a true and fair view of the operating and financial position. They are an integral part of a set of complete financial statements.

External audit A periodic examination of the books of account and records of an entity conducted by an independent third party (an auditor) to ensure that they (a) have been properly maintained, (b) are accurate and complete, (c) comply with established principles and accounting standards, and (d) give a true and fair view of the financial state of the entity.

Fair value	The U.S. Financial Accounting Standards Board's Statement of Financial Accounting Standards No. 157: Fair Value Measurements (SFAS 157) defines fair value as the price that would be received to sell an asset or paid to transfer a liability in an orderly transaction between market participants at the measurement date. By comparison, fair value is generally defined in IFRS as the amount for which an asset could be exchanged, or a liability settled, between knowledgeable, willing parties in an arm's length transaction.
Financial reporting	The presentation of financial data regarding a company's position, operating performance, and funds flow for an accounting period.
Generally Accepted Accounting Principles (GAAP)	The standards or rules preparers must follow in determining what financial information should be included in general-purpose financial statements and how it should be presented.
Generally Accepted Auditing Standards (GAAS)	A set of systematic guidelines used by auditors in conducting independent audits on companies' finances, to ensure the accuracy, consistency, and verifiability of auditors' actions and reports.
Income statement	A statement showing the revenues from business operations, expenses of operating the business, and the resulting net profit or loss of a company over a specific period of time. Also called a profit-and-loss statement. It is an integral part of a set of complete financial statements.
Independent oversight board	An entity that regulates and oversees the work of external auditors. These bodies, which have replaced self-regulation arrangements, are required in many countries, including the United States, European Union member states, and Japan.
Internal audit	A systematic process carried out by independent employees of a company to provide assurance to management and the board of directors that internal controls are adequate to mitigate risks, governance processes are effective and efficient, and organizational goals and objectives are met.

International Education Standards for Professional Accountants (IES)	A set of standards to prescribe the essential elements of education to become a professional accountant and the ongoing education requirements to remain competent. Developed by the International Federation of Accountant's (IFAC's) International Accounting Education Standards Board.
International Financial Reporting Standards (IFRS)	Formerly known as International Accounting Standards, IFRS are general-purpose corporate financial reporting standards and interpretations adopted by the International Accounting Standards Board (IASB).
International Standards on Auditing (ISA)	Professional standards of audit issued by IFAC's International Auditing and Assurance Standards Board (IAASB).
Issuer	Legal entity that is authorized to issue (offer for sale) its securities. Examples include corporations, investment trusts, and government entities.
Listed company	A company whose debt or equity trades on a regulated stock exchange. To be listed, a company normally has to meet certain financial reporting and corporate governance requirements.
Preparer	An individual involved in preparing financial statements.
Professional body	Association of an organized profession (such as accounting); frequently one that certifies successful completion of its requirements, and thereupon awards a license to practice.
Public interest entities (PIEs)	Entities that are of significant public relevance because of the nature of their business (in particular, companies whose securities are admitted to trading on a regulated market, banks, insurance companies, and other financial institutions), their size, or their number of employees.
Regulated entity or supervised entity	An entity that engages in activities that require its financial reports to be regulated by a supervisory body. Banks, listed companies, and nonbank financial institutions (including insurance undertakings, pension and investment funds, credit cooperatives, and so

forth) are typically supervised by a (separate or combined) regulatory body.

Report on the Observance of Standards and Codes (ROSC) A report that summarizes the extent to which countries observe certain internationally recognized standards and codes for data dissemination; fiscal transparency; transparency in monetary and financial policies; banking supervision; securities regulation; insurance supervision; payments and settlements; corporate governance; accounting and auditing; insolvency and creditor rights; and anti-money laundering and combating the financing of terrorism. Reports summarizing countries' observance of these standards are prepared and published by the World Bank and the International Monetary Fund at the request of the member country.

Small and medium enterprises (SMEs) Companies that are classified below a defined threshold, and as such are commonly treated differently in law or policy than larger, public-interest entities. Countries use a number of different parameters and thresholds for defining SMEs, including the total amount of assets controlled, total revenues, total borrowings, and number of employees.

Standard setter An agency, usually governmental or quasi-governmental, with the authority to set national or international standards (for example, for accounting). The International Accounting Standards Board (IASB) is an example of a recognized international standard setter.

State-owned enterprise (SOE) An enterprise in which the state has significant control, through full, majority, or significant minority ownership.

Statement of changes in equity A statement that reconciles the equity balances of an entity at the beginning and end of an accounting period. It is an integral part of a set of complete financial statements.

Supervisors or regulators Authorities charged with monitoring financial performance and operations of entities in a specific sector to ensure that they are operating in accordance with applicable rules and regulations. Most often, the following sectors are subject to supervision: banking, securities markets, insurance, and pension funds.

Tertiary education

Also called *higher* and *post-secondary* education; refers to studies following the completion of a secondary degree (for example, high school or equivalent). It may include education obtained at a college, university, or vocational school.

Index

www.ingramcontent.com/pod-product-compliance
Lightning Source LLC
Chambersburg PA
CBHW061305220326
41599CB00026B/4735